THE ART OF LIFE
LIVING TOGETHER IN HARMONY

THE TEACHERS OF THE HIGHER PLANES
Third Book of Wisdom

Ruth Lee, *Scribe*

LeeWay
PUBLISHING

Lee Way
PUBLISHING

This book is an updated and revised version of the 2005 edition originally published by AuthorHouse.

LeeWay Publishing
Naples, Florida USA
www.LeeWayPublishing.com

ISBN: 978-0-9970529-2-3
Library of Congress Control Number: 2016951903
Printed in the United States of America
First Printing 2016

Cover design by Sarah Barrie of Cyanotype.ca
Internal design by Alfredo Sarraga Jr.

More Books by **Ruth Lee**

OTHER **BOOKS OF WISDOM** FROM
THE TEACHERS OF THE HIGHER PLANES

WE ARE HERE

THE WORK BEGINS

NOW IS THE TIME

THE WORLD OF TOMORROW

BLISS IS IT!

ॐॐ

THE WORD OF THE MAYA

THE MAKING OF A SCRIBE - *HOW TO ACHIEVE A LIFE*
YOU CAN WRITE ABOUT

WRITING IN SPIRIT WORKBOOK

WRITING IN SPIRIT NOTEBOOK

CAN YOU PRAY? *WE ARE ALL HERE TO SEEK THE WAY*

ॐॐ

NOVELS BY RUTH LEE

ANGEL OF THE MAYA

WITHIN THE VEIL: *AN ADVENTURE IN TIME*

WRITING IN SPIRIT ~ *JEANNE'S STORY*

Dedicated to Ruth Lee's coaching and counseling clients whose support enabled her to produce this new edition of THE BOOKS OF WISDOM

THE ART OF LIFE
LIVING TOGETHER IN HARMONY

THE TEACHERS OF THE HIGHER PLANES
Third Book of Wisdom

Ruth Lee, *Scribe*

LeeWay
PUBLISHING

Introduction

The re-issuance of **The Books of Wisdom** from *The Teachers of the Higher Planes* marks the reopening of LeeWay Publishing, rather than a new venture.

LeeWay Publishing was created to reproduce works channeled by the extraordinary spiritual scribe, Ruth Lee, otherwise known as *The Scribe*. She alone supervised the re-publication of this work, refraining from making significant changes to the original manuscript.

From its inception, the mission of LeeWay Publishing has been to provide knowledge urgently needed to elevate the consciousness of humanity. However, long before LeeWay came into being, *The Scribe* responded positively to the request of a group of entities from higher realms known as *The Teachers of the Higher Planes* to 'trance-scribe' their works for the benefit of mankind and planet Earth.

Having been sent by a higher authority to assist all who are ready to align their potential and take effective action, *The Teachers* clearly demonstrate ways we can all heal our lives, our world, and planet Earth. Thus, *The Teachers* provide light in a time of spiritual darkness.

Of all *The Books of Wisdom*, it is **The Art of Life ~ *Living Together in Harmony*** that best describes how to dwell comfortably among others while following your personal path to success in this life and the next.

To learn more about *The Books of Wisdom, The Teachers of the Higher Planes*, and *The Scribe*, Ruth Lee, visit **www.LeeWayPublishing.com**.

Chapter One

The Art of Life is the Art of Living

You have to live before you can love. If your life is not creating a wonderful personality, you are responsible for it. You have total control of your life. Nobody else can take the blame or credit for it. You live! You work! You love! You are!

The old world belief that you must marry and merge your life with another to find soulful love is erroneous—and never believed, but the new idea of marrying many times is not any better. There are no *'soul mates'*. You are not a single entity split before birth and expected to search the world until you find your *'better half'*. You are one soul!

You are a single entity with many dimensions, and each dimension has a life of its own, but you are the only one living on Earth in this reality called life. You will not live on another planet nor soar into the stratosphere while here. You live, work, and love on Earth until you accomplish all you set out to do and can advance to the next plane.

The work of this plane is to advance you to the next one. If you dawdle and live an endless life of selfishness, you will be back. You will return to this class and be expected to honor the commitments of the life you failed, as well as those of a new life. This creates a lot of responsibility and may be reflected in many duties and worries accepted by your soul. You have the right and privilege to ignore all the spiritual gifts you may access to help you through this life—even seeking your Spiritual Guides, but you are not given credit for doing so.

We are not bothered by anyone who refuses to listen to us. We are here to help, and if it is not wanted, we do not care. If you want help, it is here for you now! If you exaggerate your need for help, we will ignore what you do not need, but will meet real needs.

When we began our work here, we often asked you to speak for the rest of us and answer for the work you do, but now we seldom speak to new generations. They do not listen to their elders. Why?

If elders of the world are unwise, they are foolish. We are not here to help fools. It is your world. You have procreated and created this world and its inhabitants, so if you love what you have made of it, you best listen now.

In the old ways the only one to believe in God was the shaman and the oldest of the population. All others sought a livelihood and sought out elders for spiritual advice. If the elders were negligent in their studies, the entire population suffered. Today, older people of your societies are not as wise. They do not study the workings of the world and God's ways of helping people accede to the desired result of winning this round of work and advancing to the next plane. If you want to learn to accede to the desired outcome of moving upward to the next plane, listen. We will offer you many ways to leave this plane and advance, which is your idea—not ours.

You must learn to curb your tendency to ignore all that requires work. If you do not work hard on your life, who will? Not us. We have a large population on Earth to attend to and help. We will never repeat a lesson or expect a lesson to be failed. It is your decision to egoistically erupt into anger or sulk if the lesson is too close to your problem. You can erupt and focus your energy on the problem or on the result, it is up to you. We care not at all about your problems, but we are here to make the final results acceptable to the Highest Guides who will sit in judgment when you cross over.

The early work of this era began some time ago, but is now stalled. It began in a haze of drugs and overtures toward the opposite sex that ended in disillusionment in relationships. We are here to help mend that work and get all back on track, as well as explain the need for relationships and why they must be worked on every day of this life.

The only work you must do now is be you!

Once you learn this lesson, you are expected to accept that others are also here to be themselves. Once you can respect that fact, the world is a shiny new top that spins in the same direction as the universe and its goals. Your work here on Earth is not the same as the universal goal of ending each life in the line of ascension to God.

You chose this work—living on Earth—in order to develop into a far higher being than you ever were before. If you fail, you may be returned to a lower level or be asked to repeat this class. Yes, this is a classroom and you are all students. No one on Earth is above anyone else as far as the elders are concerned. You may become an elder, but that is not actually why you are here.

If your life is drawn by you, colored by you, and acted out by you, who do you think is responsible for what you do? Simple answer, but you make it difficult. You often refer to the fact that you cannot do what you want to do due to restrictions and laws, but you do not change the restrictions and laws. You simply complain about them. To complain and do nothing to change whatever is the weirdest way to live. You have to hear the noise to believe it.

If you and your tribe were in charge, we think you would do exactly the same as those now in power. We see you wanting the same power, money, prestige, etc., but you do not want to follow rules. The reason you wish to lead is based on greed. You will never learn by being given money, nor will you learn by being in power. You learn by being made to work and acknowledge what others know—that work is used to pass the time from birth-to-death in as easy a manner as possible.

We are not here to dissolve the work of the world or change it in any way. We want you to change it if it is not to your liking. Since you live here and work only for you, why would we do your work? To be you is the hardest goal on Earth to achieve, and it takes a lifetime of

3

preparation to do it, but it comes to those who work and believe they are on the way to the next plane. Those who are lost or have lost their belief in God who are unable to continue—and due to the shortness of their time on Earth now distract others.

We came here today to be with you. We will leave Earth at the appointed time and never return, but you will return here until there is either no planet to return to or you are accepted into the next plane.

When you hear the world is going to end, what do you think? We sense you believe Earth will disappear from the universe, but not think it important since you will be dead by then. This idea is not the only false belief you have, but it can cost you your soul.

To listen and then question the work of others is wise, but to listen and question in order to ridicule others is unwise. We know many refuse to say what they think due to incessant ridicule. Another problem: elders are now afraid of your children. How to overcome such a ridiculous occurrence? Work at it!

Listening to some people talk about the world's problems, you might draw the conclusion that someone else is responsible. Before you agree, think of all you did to let this world descend into chaos.

1. Did you ever help another enjoy life?
2. Did you ever help a child learn a lesson in humility?
3. Did you ever teach a child how to manage anger?
4. Do you live according to the rules of your society?
5. If you are free of children, do you think you do not have to care for them?
6. Do you ever help a mother or father discipline a child who has erred?
7. Do you care?

These represent the seven deadliest sins of any society.

You must care!

If you were to die and leave all your money to your children, would it be wasted? If you say 'yes,' then spend it. If your children cannot handle their finances, the only money you should leave behind is enough to pay off all your debts and dispose of your body. No money should be left to people who care nothing about you. A fraternal organization that helps those in need would be a better place to dispose of excess riches than to leave it to children unfit to manage their own lives who would be hardened into lives of ease and disrespect.

If you were to die with many debts, would your children pay them? The average person has no debts at the end of life, but if you did, would you have the money to pay them? If not, you are living a life of greed now. You must never owe what you cannot pay back.

If you live on the earnings of another and never contribute your share, you are greedy and can expect to return to life here on Earth to earn your living in some disagreeable way. That will be the lesson of this life. Perhaps some are living such a life now?

When you live off the work of another, accept that you have no power as a result of failing to do your work. You cannot own the work of another. Never let your work suffer because you *can* fall back on the work of another. Your life is your life, and the generosity of another is not yours to claim. You will be returned to Earth to do a lot of charitable work at low pay if you live off the work of a loved one. Perhaps you are living that life now and feel you earned time off, we never judge, but *The Judges* will see that you work hard.

If your life on Earth continually grows away from God, you cannot enter the kingdom of God or even the next plane. "Let it all go," some say, but you are unwise to heed them. When the time comes to cross over, you will be far from them, because they likely learned their lesson and are on their way to glory—leaving you to pay the price for following bad advice. You cannot blame anyone for giving you misdirection. You are constantly told if you are on the wrong road, yet too many scream: "How do I know if I'm on the wrong path?" *You just know!*

The reason we are here and working together is to learn how to develop into the best entity we can b, so we can begin living together in close harmony. If the life you chose for yourself is selfish, we think you should change, but it is your choice. Since we think a selfish individual is most unlikely to change, we spend very little time and effort on such people. If you are selfish and aware of it, you should now be able to determine if you need to change.

The world is not the best place to be happy, but it is the only place you have now. You are not the only one here, but you live in the past and dwell in the future so much that you seldom live here *now*. When you live in the past, you never appreciate what you have today; and when you live in the future, you are lost to the goodness and beautiful life you have now. Such people are the fools of this world. Do you count yourself among them?

When the time comes to leave a planet and go to another life, it is often the way of natural beings to expect the next life to be better than this one, but it is not always the case. You have the ability to make sure it is, but it is your choices in this life that determine your next life. We cannot describe for you the lives you lived before this one, but before the end of our work, you will know the life you can expect on the next plane.

We are not afraid of life, but often see you shrink from knowledge of it, because you fear death. We will talk of death, as well as its effects on relationships. It is not a morbid session, but you must start growing out of such childish beliefs in order to advance to the truth.

In this world are many people who are not of God—and we know who they are. We want you to also be able to recognize them, but you are not to hold them in contempt or judge them. It is merely an exercise in becoming the best you can be while helping yourself. It always helps the work go more easily and faster if you can avoid trouble. This is the only reason we would ever want you to behave differently toward one person than toward others. Those who are not of God will stand out. You will notice a drain of energy when they are present. When the work of the soul is going great, the heart is often unable to accommodate the energy and disposes of it in inappropriate ways.

The golden rule of work: All work daily, but those who are not of God will always avoid it. They will seek out others to do the smallest chores and help no one. If this is the description of anyone with whom you work, you must step aside and let them be exposed as idlers. It is in their best interests that they be made to work.

If you cannot sit still in the presence of a person who is constantly angry, you will notice they are red or white and unable to sit still. We suggest you look carefully into their eyes to determine if they are both the same color. If the color is distinctly different and flashing out hate, you must leave them to their wrath. If their eyes are calm and steady, lift them out of their depression. Those who are depressed are temporarily out of the mainstream of God's work and unable to appreciate life. If you help them correct their bearing and head them into the world again, you will be blessed.

The blessing of the order of evil is never as great as the blessing of God, but some do attempt such silly gestures. You should be aware this automatically results in another lifetime on Earth—to learn the difference between ego and God. When the work of the ego is left to develop in a positive way, the ego of negative ones will try to dislodge the work of the Holy Spirit with spite, jokes, and other derisive attitudes, thus risk the chance of being cursed.

To be blessed is a great boon, but to be cursed by the godly is to end this life in a prison within your mind. Be cool to anyone who cannot accept changes that occur within the mind, heart, and body of those who find peace. That peace is always of God and that person is no longer anemic. You will be shot down if you try to harm a person, or image of a person, who attains the work of God.

If the day is too long and you are tired, we often ask you to sit, relax, and breathe deeply. You are not asked to meditate or develop into another aspect of your personality, and you are not expected to develop great plans and ideas, instead you need to relieve the mind and body of the pain and work of such a day. People become tired if they let their work accumulate. If you shed your work each day, it does not accumulate. If the work of the day is too much for you, or you do not like it, you will ignore people around you daily—especially those at home. We do not want this to happen.

You must work at a project or job long enough to see if it is for you, and not continue to do such work if it drains you of all that is *you*. However, the only time to seek another job is after you fully understand why you dislike the one you have. This is the only way to gain knowledge of self and succeed at the next job.

Many are rapidly changing now, unable to understand why they stayed in a bad job or sought no help. This is not the time to wish to delve into such thoughts. You have only enough time to do your work and get in the proper channel before the end of this life—so do not waste time analyzing the past. If the work of your life is not going well, you may decide another work would be easier. If so, you should do it, but it may not be work that is holding you back.

We often see you struggle with the weight of others' burdens while ignoring your own. Why do this? You have enough trouble in your life to keep your mind on track and busy. Why take on others' work? We think it is ego.

The ego is the source of evil in the world!

The ego is the source of your pain and suffering, which then develops into being the only path open for some. Why would anyone wish to suffer? You do. You often are so afraid of others that you make up stories to exploit your ego. Why? You are unsure if you are as good as other people. You are! The foolishness of ego is to wonder about who is winning or losing. You are all in the human race, and no one else is on the same track as you are now—so how can they beat you?

It is the ego of others that conflicts with your ego. You do not like to be less than others—but enjoy being more. This is your puzzle to solve! We do not care for such trivial matters, but if you require an overview, we can provide it.

The only work you are required to do is for God and You. Once you become the only one who cares about You while here and does your work, you feel the pride of knowing you can succeed on your own. If you let others work out all your problems, you will never succeed or be believed. It is not easy to let others work alone if they do it incorrectly—which is how we see you, but we must let you live your life. You cannot learn any other way.

If the major religions of the world were to unite, who would be in charge? God! The religions of the present world are governed by men who struggle constantly to be in charge. Why? Ego is the reason. When the ego is in charge of a personality, it causes that person to see things in a totally self-centered, different way. If you are ego-driven, and most of you are, the world looks bleak or dark at times. The world never changes color or demeanor. You are who changes.

If the religions of the world never united, the work of God would still exist. Why? God is not in your ego! God is within your Spirit or soul—and you never give up your soul. You can give up ego for a time, but never your soul. Once the soul changes, it stays that way, but the ego can vacillate from one pole to another. It is that way so you can learn about ego and such things while here.

To demand one person worship in one church rather than another is the way of the ego—not God. The worship of God is not continued and carried through better by one group rather than another. It is best done individually, but as a group you may be able to do more in the world.

When you discover the light of God, you can finally see. Before the light there is no darkness, rather a dimming of all human senses when pride rules. You need to be *you*, but it is not a prideful endeavor. The wisdom of your spiritual self must be allowed to control your life—not the vanity of your ego.

When you are within the light of God, you can see God is. You know it. You exist. You believe. Your life is completely turned into the life you always dreamed you would have someday. Why wait until someday for that life?

We will continue this discussion in the next chapter, now we have an exercise for you to do before you advance.

EXERCISE YOUR RIGHTS

1. Imagine your life exists in a basket. Is it overflowing or barely visible? If your basket is not heaped above the top, place more love into your work. Gain insight into the real *you*. This is a visualization exercise designed to help you gain insight into how you are developing your life.
2. To put your life in perspective, visualize a clock with the hands set at high noon to represent the end of your work. If the hands are quickly approaching high noon, know you have little time to waste. Only if your life is in order and you have enough time can you help others, otherwise do not worry about anyone else right now.
3. Seek out a doctor or nurse and ask them about the nature of disease. See if they believe medicine has all the answers. You should be convinced by now that life is not to be left to doctors, but is your responsibility. If you can understand how little medicine has to do with health, you may learn to develop your body.
4. Once you know the work of a day is over, sit and meditate on what you accomplished. Was it worth the labor? Did it improve your life? Was it dull or boring? Were you gainfully employed or merely making a living? When you clearly see the answers, ask yourself: Why would anyone want this life? If the answer is: I am happy or completed by it—or words to that effect, continue doing it. However, if your answer reflects that you feel negative about your work, start changing it now.
5. If each day's work is unworthy of you, you will never work hard, which is not the best way to spend this life. Begin exercising your power to develop yourself rather than work for anyone who would not let you fully develop. If your help is

unnecessary, you never feel accomplished or accepted, so get another line of work.

6. You need to be busy, active, and love what you do to be *you*. Living any other way is not worth the life it saps from *you*. You must exercise your right to be *you*!

This is the last phase of this work and its effect on *you*. You have only enough time to do one work well. What will it be? The only work worthy of *you* is work you do well, so get on with it!

Chapter Two

During this session we will delve into the work of partners and why they are important if you intend to develop and become the best you can be. The work itself is not as important as the level of cooperation achieved. This is what we mean: *A partnership is the ultimate relationship.*

If you cannot work or live with another, you are at the end of life here. You will be unable to endure life in this world since it is established as a means to an end—to live cooperatively as one family or tribe. If a tribe is of great size, you will be reduced by several generations, but that would be the only dimensional change. *(This puzzles The Scribe, so let us describe it better.)*

If you have a large clan and must ask for approval of your plan before you can pursue it, you lose a lot of time—maybe several generations to complete it. This is not the same as saying you have to marry if you expect to go to the next plane. This means you must learn to live together and devote a portion of your time to helping others. If you have no vested interest in anyone else, you likely never help others, which results in isolation. Interdependence could not develop beyond the outer edges of your personality.

This book is not about love or being human. It is about achieving the state of being *you*—becoming *you* by helping others. It would be easy to say you are *you*, if you know who you are, but alas you do not know that. The only way you can see yourself is by watching or checking your reflection in a mirror or in the eyes of others. If you could act and see exactly what is wrong before going further, that would be the best of all worlds, but not possible on this plane.

Your life is not as easy to run and maintain as it once was. You now have many difficult days due to this world's technology interfering with your life. You can no longer act spontaneously. You can no longer act independent of all others, nor can you see yourself as you are.

Others sharing your space are only interested in themselves. You asked for space and were granted space in which to investigate your needs. Now what do you do with it?

The only other world you know—the land of dreams—is seen in fractured dimensions and unclear to you, thus not a way to reflect on your present life. Although it does not reflect the life you live now, it is helpful when used to explore You *(the Higher Self)*. Dreams help you deepen the connection between *you* and your psyche, but seldom help you understand why you do not get along with others. The realm of ego is hard to understand without someone around to help you. We will help you now, but later you must seek wisdom from others in your world.

When you cannot understand life, you often blame people who raised you—regardless of the lapse of time. If you are over age 21, this is absurd. You no longer owe your parents anything but respect; but if your parents raised you to the best of their ability, you have much to be grateful for now. If they foolishly wasted your time together, you may have learned more than others. It is not the time you spent alone in youth, but the time you spend helping others *now* that determines whether you are fit to advance.

What you need to do to advance your life is to work as others do until you know who you are—then get your own work. If you enjoy another's work, an apprenticeship is the best way to learn, but that means of teaching is seldom used anymore. Why? Perhaps everyone values the dollar more than the work? It is often said that greed is caused by people who do not want to work, preferring others to do work that pays them. We are unsure if that accurately reflects the ethic of today's workforce, but in many ways that we observed it is appropriate.

You need to develop your spiritual work, but how can you do that if you do not work? Your life is a series of discoveries and choices. Once work is discovered, you choose to do it or not. If you do not tell us what you want to do, we will be unable to help you with your work.

The only ones who can carry out the work of your soul are those who love you—and those people are not required to do so. You are! If your love of self is so great that others are repelled, you will receive no help. You alone have to do your work, which results in learning much.

We could object to the way you act, but not to the final outcome. At the end of this dateline you call life, you will find answers to all your questions, but you need time now. Your life is not as interesting to anyone else as it is to you, and once you discover this truth, your life is much easier to live.

If you do not work, we will not help you develop. We are not interested in you if you lack interest in who we represent. We are not human, but certain principles are true of all nature.

In your words, ask us how to handle the biggest problem in your life. Is it the time you lost or the times you won? The work of this world is about losses! In order to exact from these lessons all the work you need, begin with an early loss and work up to today. What else taught you more? Nothing! Your life is not made up of losses, but you remember them best.

According to others, what are your biggest wins? Why? Were you on your own or working in a group then? Were you the star or a supporting cast member? You are never remembered by others for what you did alone. You are remembered by those in the same cast or group. They are the only ones who remember you—and only what you did with them.

Your family will be there for you, but only if you remember to help them. They do not need help, but you should give it from time-to-time to show you care. It is the only human way available to spread your energy to those important to you. If you need help, how many outside your family will help you? If you think many will help, you are mistaken. A family is your insurance policy against old age, deterioration of health, and loss of work. We suspect many are beginning to realize this is true, but why would you doubt it?

In this world are many who doubt everything. They sap the energy of all who work or live around them. Since you are not encouraged to be with them, you avoid and neglect them. We suggest you try to ignore their complaints and help them develop a better attitude. If you do, you will notice they are not as ignorant nor do they complain as much. It is hard to be ignorant and complain about the only people who care about why you are here.

If you know worldly ones who are unhappy, why do you think you would be happy with their lives? We often watch in amazement as you view the lives of those supposedly rich and famous, envying their homes, cars, or beauty. What would you do differently to be happy? Would you buy more? Entice more people into your family circle? Invest in another way of life? What would you do, if not be you?

These days are the end of time for this world. Almost everything has been tried by someone. If what was attempted succeeded, it is already a part of this life.

It is your nature and ego that defines you. If you wish to be different, you do not need money to change, but you need to work. Most say to work on your own life is boring. To them, working on others is much more interesting. Why? Because they do not have to do the work.

Work is hard. Work can be boring and tedious, but work is how you get to be *you!* No one else cares if you do or do not become all you can be, but us—and your mother.

We are not afraid of the dark, but too many of you are. Why? Darkness is not evil or difficult to navigate when your technology is as advanced as it is now, so why not live during the darkest hours of the day? We suspect you do not feel as good when the sun is not shining, and we may be right. The sun is power, energy, and warmth. It causes the body to exert itself more, and in its own way develop into another person once you decide to change. If your life work is hastened by the sun, seek it out.

If you hate the dark and cannot stand the sun, when do you live? No one works on the side of the moon you do not see from the light side. You exist in the dark exactly as you do in the day, so why believe strange things happen only at night? This is superstitious beliefs of idiots or unenlightened people.

You are of the new age and able to determine what is true or false—right? Wrong! You are still the same as you were in distant times—only now you have computers. Computers are banks of information about people, times, and places not needed now. You will remember all you need to know when you cross over to the other side. To save all this data is like watching a pack rat save foil and string. When will the rat ever need it or retrieve it? What good will it be if it is retrieved? It is merely an exercise in keeping the population busy. We see that—why cannot all of you see it, too?

To work on one project all your life, then see it destroyed right before you die would be frustrating, but you work on nothing all your life. You do not attempt to prepare for death or the next life. Why? Do you seriously believe someone will come along and save *you* from death? We think you know it is not to be, but if you do not know it by now—it is not to be. We all know that!

Listen to your body. It is here for you to use, but not abuse. If you abuse your body, it will react and retaliate as if of its own will. We are not here to say your body cannot act of its own accord. The body is not a mechanical tool or beast of burden. It needs help to determine the right food and drink. It is not easily killed, but will die if left to do so. You are the brain. If you decide to load yourself with toxic waste, drink substances that destroy tissue, or breathe impure air, but who are you killing?

To kill the self is the purest form of evil ever devised by the human race. We see it done in many shapes and forms. You are now aware of the destruction smoke does to the air and lungs, yet you all prevent changes necessary to clear the air all over the world. You say others are at fault, but you do not do anything concrete to help clear it now. Trees are needed to clean the air, but you burn them. Trees are needed for erosion control, but you cut them down and do not leave enough growing to hold back rains. Since greed and studied stupidity is at fault, why do all of you pretend you do not mind and it is okay to do it?

This is a book about relationships—and Earth is the host upon which all of you live. It is the primary relationship upon which all life is formed. If you destroy it, you will have no further relationships here. We are not harping about destroying rain forests in other countries, because we see all countries guilty of destroying forests and reducing them for the sake of grand estates and small houses. So much arable soil in one country has been plowed under to build houses that if it becomes necessary for those people to return to agriculture, they could not raise enough crops to feed their population. Why would any thinking people do this?

Your life is not as you think it is or think it was. It is a series of recollections and beliefs—none of which are accurate. The work of a few provides brief glimpses into the lives of others, so some try to become writers and artists in order to capture their lives or faces the same way, but that seldom works. No one cares about knowing you. All want to know about themselves—not you. So if you would be remembered after leaving Earth, write about or picture people who cannot represent themselves—give them names and faces easily recalled—then *you* will be remembered.

When the world is gone, completed, and not to be repeated, we will help *The Judges* sift through the remains to determine what was worth all this trouble. We feel sure it will be the few who learned God exists in everything they do, see, and work on now. We do not see many of you believe in God and the work you do, let alone what you want for others. You cannot dwell on the needs of others when not *you*, but once *you*, welcome the work of others and help them learn who they are, too.

Whatever you do—do it well. Once you do a great job, you will see work is not as difficult as it would be if done half-heartedly. That is when you know life is only as difficult as you make it.

In this world are many who would be kings and queens, but nobody wants kings or queens now. So why would so many want to be royalty? To lord it over others that they are superior is the reason; but who is superior? Not anyone we have seen. All of you are flawed and damaged. None of you has great lasting beauty or features of stone. You all have to pay for your life, so be glad it is as good as it is. Forget the realm of royalty, it never earned its keep and deserves little respect. *You* of the spiritual realm are who work and deserve the respect of those who follow after you in times to come.

If life is not as easy to understand as it would be if you had a friend or lover, we want to know why you lack definition. Why would anyone else add life to your existence? If you are less a person without another around you, how can you live with yourself?

Examine the tapes you play and believe! Your belief system created these tapes and they reflect your mind. Do you truly believe you can only be happy if you have a partner? Think of all the things you do alone and cannot do with another. How many people are you? Do you think you could be more than you are if you had to share this *you* with others?

In life, as you know it, there are many who live for the time when they will be alone—and we often wonder about this. Why would the absence of another be uplifting? You need other people, and you need time alone, but to abuse that time worrying about others is not the best use of your life. We would like to see you enjoy yourself regardless of whether or not others are nearby. We think it is possible and probable that you feel the same way, too. For this reason, we continue to explore the various ways you control your life.

The following exercise is meant to develop self-control. You may take as long as needed to do it, but it must be completed before you continue to the next chapter.

AN EXERCISE IN SELF CONTROL

1. On the first of each month list what needs to be done that month and do the first day's chores that day. If you are now midway between months, begin today. Do you want the work completed? Do you feel it is important? Do you do it because others think it is important? Do you do it merely to support work of another? If you work to help another, give yourself a star. If you do it only because you believe it should be done, give yourself a demerit. Add up all assets or stars and deduct demerits. Anything on the plus side is a keeper.

2. As you do that work, put your life in order. Small or large tasks makes no difference, but each must be done. Place the biggest events in one column, then in a column opposite list small things that helped make it happen and those who helped you. Do you owe more than you thought possible? If you did this correctly, the answer is "yes". Sit down and determine how to recommend each person for a better life or help them yourself.

3. On a list of names you prepare for mailing greetings, scratch out anyone well-known to you. If you find you do not really know any of them, why send personal greetings? Either get to know them or make new friends. Life is too short to continue sending messages without renewing relationships.

4. Take friends to lunch or dinner, better yet, make lunch or dinner for them. If this is impossible, you are not trying to be a friend. Accept it, then proceed to the next item.

5. Tour the area where you live and spot how many people you know. Do you know fewer than five? Do you know any neighbors by their first name and have knowledge of their lives? Can you easily seek help from any neighbor? If the answers are 'no', begin searching for answers in the next chapter.

6. The teeth of a comb are evenly spaced, but your life is not. You may find several people of like-mind here or there, and then no one you like for quite some time. Would you risk losing a friend if you knew you would not find a replacement for years?

7. Place the name of each friend on a 3x5 inch card and write down all their likes and dislikes, family members, etc. If you need to fill out more than one card front and back for a person,

you see them as a friend. If you do not know enough to cover one card, discard it from the stack. You should have a good friend for every five years of your life (age 25 = 5 good friends). If friends left and were not replaced, work on meeting new people now—and being less aggressive in your irritation level.

8. Place your friends' names in a bowl, then pull out one name each day until all are called or written to at least once. If the message you deliver is obviously not welcomed, then find another friend. If your message is welcomed and reciprocated, you are back together.

These are a few ways to explore long-established friendships, but you need to remain open to developing new relationships, too. All people are changing—and need to change, but not all relationships can handle change.

Make sure your life is supported by sound friendships and good people. You must be honest and truthful, but not to the extent it damages others' egos or disrupts their lives. If you are free of such complaints, you have many friends now.

Chapter Three

The only day of your life you can say: *"I am the only one"* is the day you die. Every other day involves others. You are never the only one to be considered and never the only one who matters. If you live your life like you are *the only one*, the world will drop a bomb on you—when you can least afford it.

There is no room for roaming raiders and cut-throat warriors now. The world is too over-populated and densely built to permit such displays of individualism. Now the achiever must do it in a smaller space with more people—or not succeed.

The gift of organization is that it is fairly easy to acquire, but requires the *'organizer'* to first contain oneself. The only one who remains on top is the last one up the ladder—not the first. In other words, if young and those above you are older, you can reach the top, so it is unwise to conduct a bloodbath getting there. It would in time result in your demise, because you cannot succeed if no one is there to support you.

You say the work world is not a place for soft-hearted people. But why? Why would anyone want to work where people are less than human?

This is the myth: You work hard all day in a place where everyone seeks only money, and at the end of each day everyone goes home and complains.

This is the reality: You do not work hard enough all day to experience deep thinking, and when you arrive home you are not exhausted. The reality does not match the myth. Why?

In the world of business and industry many people work together to achieve a common goal: Success for the company that employs them all. What about other companies? They, too, seek the same goal. This produces competition, which kills cooperation. This happened in industrial cities. Everyone became so competitive they refused to drop that attitude once at home. They sought fiefdoms they could protect from *them,* carrying out isolation tactics rather than enlarging their lives through cooperation. This form of paranoia resulted in the suburbs of today.

If you read newspaper articles about crime and say, *"How can anyone live in the city?"* You are an offender and must learn to instead say: *"I wish I lived in the city."* Only then can cities be cleared of negativity.

The cities of this world are not bad! People are bad, but conditions do not induce such evil. Ego induces evil. Those who work are the only ones who desire a better place to live. Once evil is allowed to roam freely—as it is in many countries, the city is no place to remain.

Why would you let a few run wild? You would never let a mad dog roam the streets, but let insane people idle and carouse on corners where children play. This is an insane way to direct life. You must take charge and organize your society or it will be destroyed from within—quickly.

Once a city begins to return to its former status, the world does not say, *"Look, there is a success story!"* The world fears such transformation. The work of many is to destroy the old in order to rebuild. For example, it is the biggest business in America.

Rebuilding is never the answer! You need to concentrate on managing what you have and add to it as you can afford to do so. Buying and selling in order to afford something newer is living in a fool's paradise. Before you are ready, the bill must be paid.

You can improve your city!

You possess energy, power, and a positive attitude. If not, you would not be studying this book. We need you to contact others of like-mind and begin organizing and developing better plans. Once you all have a good plan, it is easy to compromise. Compromise is the cement of relationships. To compromise, you need to work on your own plan first, and once it is good in your estimation, others can tinker with it. If others want you to shed a surface detail, fine. If they want you to alter the basic premise, say no. You can define your life by the plans you make. It is a concrete way to see who you are today.

In any neighborhood there are those who choose to be different in a negative way. Why? Why would you live where you are not welcome, or your ways are not accepted or adopted? To change your neighborhood, live as you would want others to live. If your way is clearly better, they will copy you or move away. If your way is not up to the standards of others, your property value will drop.

Tenants often complain about landlords, but they are seldom realistic in what they think can be changed. Why? The tenant's envy of the owner is often so intense it cannot be eliminated from the conflict. If a tenant, you must learn to arrest your envy before deciding if the property is less in value than is charged. If it is, move. If your home is humble, but all you can afford, accept it—at least for now.

Landlords are often disgusted with tenants who do not pay for what they leased, thus taking drastic measures to insure it does not happen again—and that is the end. Why not let tenants know they cannot live rent-free and tell the world they skipped out without payment? You often cover for others who do wrong, because you do not pay for it. If you do not speak of it, how would anyone know if someone is unwilling to pay rent?

Forming a union of landlords designed to tell one another about people who destroy property is not a form of masquerade for people trying to take over the world. The landlord serves a purpose. To feed and clothe a family requires much money, thus many have no money to buy a house, so they rent. If the landlord is not treated with respect, as is apparent in cities around the world, the homes for poor people decrease until the government has to supply them.

If your country and government is selfish and desires to control all you own and will ever have, it taxes you unjustly. If your government wishes to organize huge expenditures necessary to build public works for everyone's use, it taxes you for those projects. What happens is you let others tax you in order to earn a living. This is not the place to go into taxation, but if you want a project to work on that would benefit everyone in your country, why not work on tax reform?

If you need the benefits of government, do you need a job? Your job can be used to help others or not, but it is your job to make a living for yourself. Once a job is important to you, it is important to everyone. No one's work is unnecessary. If you work and all around you do not, what happens to you? You become lazy, too. Watching others sit and do nothing is a terrible way to live. You can ignore it, but the work of your day is to be busy.

In a village all contribute to the diversity of the countryside. If the village has no one to perform a certain necessary work, someone will learn or an outsider will enter the circle and do it. If all work is done and no one else is needed to enter the circle, in time people leave and form another village. This is fine. This is worthwhile.

Why would you contribute to paying for work no one needs? For example, farmers who no longer sell their produce can become artisans. Artisans whose work is not liked change their style. It is no big deal to change your work. You are not made of concrete or brick. You need only retool and begin again on new work. Work changes as you age, regardless of who you are or where you work. The strength of youth gives way to the wisdom of age, and the need to exert power wanes. We want you to defend the job you do, but move on if it changes you too much.

In the world of those who live in difficult climates, many change drastically to suit the weather. This is considered to be wise. But if you constantly change, how do you return to the original? You do not. You may revise and alter, but to change back to the original would result in a loss.

To alter, revise, and live is the way of life. To adapt is another way of living—which is good. All adapt and live. You cannot remain in the womb or playpen. Explore, experience, and learn whatever you want to know. You are never told what you must do. This is not the time to develop a learning theory, but maybe as time goes by we will do that, too.

You want to construct a life of ease in the world for yourself, but who will do your work? We see you never worry about that, nor who you might harm in order to develop your work. Remember, you must never harm another. This is a fundamental behavior necessary to avoid being shipped back when you cross over. If you act like you are the only person alive, you will be shipped back!

No one owes you anything!
You, however, owe everything to others

What you do to Earth is your way of acting like a powerful person— and it may reflect badly on you. You may look like a ravaging pig or a brutal stalker to those above. You need to think of the impression you make on your young and be aware of others who also impress them. The impression or image you make is what is seen—not *you*. Since the real *you* remains unknown, how you act now is how *you* appear to be.

We never act in discord with our inner selves—nor do you. The only way to begin a life of ease is to first work for it. Once you achieve a level of comfort above the level of others, you may desire to live elsewhere. This is not a wise thing to do. You are better off living among peers. To enjoy the fruits of your labor, you need to compare yourself to others. If you gather together with those who are retired, having achieved much elsewhere, you never know how well you did compared to how they lived their lives.

The work of the world is not the only work you must do. You may not realize the work of *The Scribe* is such that she is busier now than when she worked in the world. She is much busier! How can that be? We know of many people who are not working now, but keeping busy. How can you be busy yet never work? It is so easy that most of you are guilty of it. Live and work, but do not work merely to keep busy.

Creating a theory or plan is developing an idea that may take many hours of work. To sit and hack apart others' ideas and plans is not work. You need to learn to sit and debate. If you debate issues and listen to what others say, you learn. If you ask questions, you never learn more than those answers. You need to ask questions, of course, but not to the extent many do now.

Listening is hard work, but talking is seldom work. You need to develop a way to listen as you work. If you can do both at the same time, the work goes much faster. If you listen to your Spiritual Guides, you feel a certain peace enter your heart and your hands fly as you work. If you listen to soft, relaxing music, your ears open and your mind is at ease. If you are unable to listen, you become tight and tense.

Whatever you do to work in the world, you alone do it. You are expected to handle the area you are assigned. If you cannot or will not do it, you must inform those who assigned the work to you. We cannot expect all work be done well, but we can expect it will be done right once you accept it. If you cannot do it, you are reliable only if you tell those who assigned the work that you cannot complete it. If you do not, you are unreliable!

The worst offense to any Organization is to be unreliable

If your work this life is not reliable or organized, you may learn much by working in an organization or associating with orderly people. However, if basically unreliable about everything, you will not learn correct ways, thus need to be disappointed. Once a person experiences disappointment, the act of disappointing others is less and less appealing to the offender.

We are not here to hire you, but do you appear at work ready for work? The only people who can work are those prepared to do it. If you act like you are ready to start work immediately, but you are not, you will be asked to leave soon after starting the job. Why would you do this to *you* and organizations that believe in you?

To state honestly you want work is never wrong. To say you want work, but only wish to make money is wrong. In some areas the odd way of employing people is so unreliable that many are hired to do work a few can easily handle in half the time allotted. Before you sit down to hire someone to work for you, listen to the Guides present and ask if work is to be done by one or several seeking the position.

The work of Guides is to employ and help people develop on this plane. You need Spiritual Guides if you employ people. In the only other area where people constantly need to develop along with their surroundings, work is assigned.

You need to develop all the time you are in school. You must learn! If you are to succeed, you must be able to get along with all who are around you. To bait those who are smaller or dumber is stupid. One day you will be in the same position.

There are many in the world of education who are not good teachers. We see them enter that work with their eyes only on money. This is not the way to teach children about ethics. You need high-minded and educated people if you expect that of your children.

Teaching is not a career. It is a calling or profession. It does not promise great money or fame, but usually results in a comfortable lifestyle and great prestige. To pay higher and higher salaries to attract teachers is the dumbest thing yet. The ones *called* to teach will do it regardless of the salary, but high wages attract all—even pederasts and other deviants you would rather not have around children. The salary does not insure the education. You insure the education! You are responsible for it.

Your children and children you care about all need you to be a party to the process. If a parent is not interested in the child, no other adult is likely to be interested, either. We see too many exacting parents who do not care about the child—only themselves. Why have children if you do not intend to help them live? After all, you had help.

You belong to a social order imposed upon you, but adults have the power and duty to change it if it harms anyone. You are not alone if you suspect Today's social order has gone far off track. It is so far from perfect that you could spend your entire life trying and not getting one car back on track. If everyone works—and works together, the train and track could be ready today.

Why do you hesitate to work together? Because you do not want to work! You want glory, fame, and fortune, but no work. The time to work is never out of style, but the time for you to work is quickly ending. You cannot work once it becomes foreign to your nature. If you let it develop into an area where you have no knowledge, you will suffer. If all of society lets that happen, you all suffer.

Today, all of you say computers rule your lives. How can a machine do that? You are becoming helpless and lazy if you believe you cannot run such machines. You need to develop your mind and attitude to accommodate them.

Whenever a person acts like the end of life is here for them, you will see it is. You need not activate any *'death cell'* or deliver a dose of poison. They did it to themselves. To live requires interest in others. If you care only about yourself, it is not long until you are either insane or dead.

Why would you prefer being insane?
Because you need not work then!

In this world of work are many who rebel each and every day and reap the rewards of idleness, but seldom believe what befalls them then is their fault. You must learn to accept the fact that work is why you came to Earth.

In the work of this world are many kinds of people who do not know their work or how to get along with others of different backgrounds. This is the reason to work in diverse places and organizations. It teaches tolerance and helps you develop into the best possible person while here.

Your present work is not the only work you can do, but if it employs you, and your mind is not idle, we suggest you stick with it. If you decide to leave this work for a different type of employment, be sure you secure new work before you leave what you do now. You would be foolish to simply leave and then worry about finding work later. This has resulted in self-destructive tendencies of men who never settled down to one job or one wife, which in turn resulted in many family breakdowns.

The family is not the only relationship where you can learn to be yourself, but it is your first experience exerting your personality and seeing how well it fits in with others, though you may not know yourself during the time you live at home. Many people need to get out among others to find out what they believe and why they are the way they are. We would expect you to let others develop, as you are not the only one with a life, but most people try to interfere with the development of another at some time in their life. May it be only for a short time!

You are not the only one with a life, but your life is the only one you have. We want you to ignore the rest if it hurts your development. If you learn and adapt, you can be supported in your ways and helped, but if not allowed to enter the family circle, it may harm your self-esteem.

Self-esteem is the key word today...Why?

'If you love and respect yourself, who can help you do more?' We see too many people making money from this old saw that we wonder who invented it. When you love yourself, you have doubts. You have wondered many times why you do things that are not *you*, so keep trying to be You. The day is not over, so you can begin again.

You need to explore and decide what is best for you, which necessarily results in mistakes—but so what! We want you to have the life you deserve. If you deserve more than you have, we will give you more. If you have more than you deserve, the world will take it away.

The term *'self-esteem'* is never applied to anyone who is successful. Why? Because such people display *self-esteem* or would not be seen as a success in these times. If you do not feel like yourself, change until you do. That makes sense, but to change in order to feel better about yourself does not. You are only here to learn. You are not here to perfect a life, but to live now. If your life were one long string of successes, how would you learn?

In the work of others we see many who would like to be you. Why? Why would someone else want your life, yet you do not? The envy and jealousy of this time is so great that many claw at others to steal their work and rewards. We will never stand back and let another steal your rewards, but you will be stripped of all you take from others, too.

If your daughter is a beauty, would you change her face? We see many mutilate and destroy a child's beauty in order to achieve social status or promote the career of a child so you need not work as hard. We will never let that go without noting it on your record. You owe your child the chance to discover why she or he is here. If they decide to change themselves later, it is their choice—not yours.

If the son of a wealthy man is given much money, is he being prepared for a life of ease? No, he is being given an opportunity to learn how to manage and create. If he misses this chance, it is his lost opportunity—not society's or yours. We would expect a son of a wealthy man to have opportunities to explore his father's work before such largess is bestowed, but that is seldom true. If the son is a wastrel, this is the fault of the father not the son.

To tempt another is to exert pressure with the desire to see that person fail. You are not to ever tempt others; but if you are tempted, your work is not to suffer. Work is always there. It never disappears.

Your children are not slaves, but are to be instructed in how to take care of themselves in all ways. The mother who does everything, for example, is not teaching respect for life. She is making her family helpless. Why would you teach nothing to a child in your protection? Ego! You want to be known as a great woman or man. You want others to think you are the only one on Earth able to have such a beautiful family and home, but no one cares. Only your children remain from the life you live now as a family. All material goods fade or break, but the love of family and responsibilities that cement it together as a union remain long after all others fail you.

Weakness is not the fault of the *tempter*—rather the *temptee*. You may not realize you are weak until tempted; nevertheless, the *tempter* is not to be blamed. Many men fail at fidelity in marriage and everyone blames the other woman. Why? The man knew what he had, she did not. If he valued his wife and family, he had a responsibility to maintain his standards. If he no longer cares for them, he believes he has the right to be himself and seek out another who is more understanding. If he has no intention of marrying the other, he has committed a sin against all. If his life is completely changed by this relationship, he has committed no sin against anyone—provided the change is for the better.

We seek out all who defame others and then do the same thing. The only words said about another should be positive or instructive. If a person does evil and you know it for a fact, you are educating all when you warn others away from that one. To warn others away from someone who has done you no harm, and you know of no harm they may have done another, you are a slanderer and will be caught. Your life will be judged the same as you judge others—that is a fact of this life.

If you slander all you meet—and many do, you never find friends. If you wish to make friends, you must talk about people in a positive manner. If you constantly attack everyone you know, no one wants to be the next one on your list.

Before leaving this subject, you must learn to develop a new face— one that smiles and is not constantly stern. If your face smiles at least half the time, you learn to act accordingly. If your face smiles all the time, you never learn how much you could do if others took you seriously. Be calm and cool, but smile. It does you and the world a lot of good.

Here are exercises to develop happy ways that promote friendship with others. Before we begin, stop now and meditate for a short time.

EXERCISES IN HAPPINESS

1. The first thing to do each morning is yawn to put your mouth in its widest, most open position. This broadens your attitude and warms up the muscles used to smile. It leads to a full grin that warms all who see you then. At first meetings—smile, then let your face soften into a more sober expression. Do not grimace.
2. The only time to ever speak ill of another is when you *know* that person did evil. Stop talking about anyone until you are capable of editing their comments before they make them.
3. Change yourself in some small way today. Take time to realize how difficult it is to change. Once you know, stop and think before asking another to change.
4. Set out a card or vase of flowers to let others see how much you care about the environment where you live and work. If you cheer others, they will cheer you.
5. Enter a contest with yourself to see how many times you say "I" in one day. Once you have the first Grand Total, reduce that number until you seldom refer to yourself. Let others speak of you—not you!
6. In the early part of each day be as stern as necessary, later on act less severe. It is important to relax and resume your usual ways before leaving the schoolroom or workplace to return home to live with your family.
7. The only time to remain alone is when you intend to meditate or work on you, otherwise welcome all who approach you.

These are a few small ways designed to change your demeanor and behavior. You will change and deliver a message to others while making them. Your outward manner reflects the inner peace of your soul. Be sure you act like *you*. It is the only way to live today.

Chapter **Four**

The date you decide to be *you* should be emblazoned on a tee-shirt, because that is your *'re-birth date'*. Never let anyone else tell you when, how, and where you may be *you*, just do it!

The time to be you is now!

The work of this world is to determine who you are and why you are, but it can lead many into a quagmire of discontent and disillusionment. Be careful of the ways of the world. You need to be aware you are not the only one traveling in this sphere. You will be among a host of others who survive and move on to the next plane, so do not enter into a competition here.

You need to develop spiritually. This entails a certain degree of psychic development as well, but some become so engrossed in psychic work that they forget to develop spiritually. You can tell if you are *'plateaued'* or stagnant by the way your work moves.

If you cannot seek help now, you need it! If you seek help and it is not forthcoming, you do not need it. The end result of such a survey is to determine where you are and why you need to help yourself. Once you determine how your life stands, you can move into the life of another and help them, but not before then. No one needs help from someone who is in deeper trouble than they are, because it can result in a double drowning.

If your life is trouble-free, begin adding to it and stirring the pot. It may bubble up and boil over, but so what? You need to be *you!* If your life is beginning to look like you, add texture and elements of risk to find out how big you can be. Adding one other person to your life involves adding a number of smaller species attached to that person. After adding up everything about that person, do you find it overwhelming or see it as a challenge? If your heart is involved, you will accept the most arduous of changes in stride; if not, you will balk at adding a single person with no family. It all depends on you.

In the species of a family tree or a single being is the making of that person. If you cannot accept the outgrowth, you cannot accept the inner person. We want you to describe the following people in your life:

- **Mother** – Who is she? Why is she still important to you?
- **Father** – Does he participate in your life? Is he still important?
- **Sisters** – Ever see them? Enjoyed them lately? Care about them?
- **Brothers** – In their lives now or not?
- **Aunts and Uncles** – Involved in their lives or not?
- **Grandparents** – Alive or dead? Indifferent or loving?
- **In-Laws** – A pretend-to-be-family or not? In your life or out of it?
- **Friends** – How many? How close? How often are you in contact?
- **Boss** – Respected? Liked? How many?
- **Co-Workers** – Liked? Would they willingly come to your wedding?
- **Children** – The biggest challenge of all!

Once you can determine the relationship of your prospective partner with these key people in *his or her* life, compare each of them to yours. Do you see any patterns or similarities between you? Do you know why some are liked or disliked and others are not? This is the time to determine if you can handle all the people who will enter your life if you get involved. You must do it if you are to have a full life together. You cannot shove them all into a closet and ignore them for the rest of your time on Earth.

If the work you do on you conflicts with *the other's* work, do you feel conflicted and bitter about it? We want you to notice how you compare your family to *the other's* family. Do you perceive irregularities in his or her family, but accept as human the foibles of your relatives? You will have trouble if you do! You need to be even more tolerant of backgrounds other than your own if it is to develop into a successful lifelong partnership.

At the end of this book list the titles of books you can access at the local library to develop your social perspective and psychology relative to living with others. We suggest you seek books that can help you understand your life now. Once you study the basics of social psychology you need only brush up on it from time-to-time as more is learned about the psychology of relationships,. If you never studied psychology, and have had problems with relationships in the past, you already know to include other areas of study, too.

To decide you cannot determine your life and relationship to another because there are so many other people involved is to admit you do not care enough to pursue the subject. Heed this warning: If your heart is not involved, you cannot continue to get involved with other people. If you do, your life will become a living hell and you will suffer.

In the list of titles you create at the end of this book, include a few books that have been around for ages—because wisdom is not likely to go out-of-style. Read and reread anything that helps you develop your personality so it more easily accepts your spiritual nature. If your life is becoming unglued or you do not know which direction to take, you need to think.

Reading presents you with facts and gives you the best opportunity to think! If your reading is sporadic, your growth is also uneven. You need to develop a routine wherein you are always reading and studying life. If you stop your education upon leaving school, you remain that age the rest of your life. We see many of you as teenagers—mentally, even though 40 years of age or older—and that is most unattractive!

Whatever you do, enter a race with every intention of winning it. Never enter a competition if you think you cannot win, because it is too demoralizing. You need to believe you stand a chance at winning the prize. If you win—great! If you do not, so what. You are who gains by trying, but will lose if you set yourself up to fail. We want you to win or at least try—but not try to lose.

If your life is not as growth-oriented as the lives of many around you, you can gain ground rapidly once you take the first step toward moving ahead. If your life is growth-oriented and you live among ignorant people and prefer to remain that way, life is a challenge—yet all the more worthwhile if you strive to win this game of life.

Select a day when you can do things for you alone. If you have no such time available now, determine why and correct it. We want you to always have time to develop and will help you make that time available now.

TIME MANAGEMENT EXERCISE

Visualize each of the following:

- Put all of your work in a basket, then place the basket on the floor.
- Place your life in another basket and put it beside the work basket.
- Arrange a bouquet of roses in the center of each basket. Which basket's blooms look best?
- The rose blooms in your *life* basket should appear brighter. If this is not the case—and your *work* basket blooms are brighter, you are wasting your life on work.
- Now put your arms around yourself and hug yourself tightly for as long as possible, then release.
- Life is not for the weak or faint-hearted, rather for the strong and stubborn, so live each day to the fullest—in every possible way today.

The time you spend on work or with others is not nearly as important as the time you spend with You (The Higher Self). How can

God enter the heart of anyone so preoccupied with others or work that he or she cannot understand that these are merely today's preoccupations.

When you live as you are, *you* really live! If you live for others, you may feel great and be admired, but what happens to the rest of your life once they move on to other things? Would you want them to always stay with you? Not if you love them. Share others' lives, but do not consume them. Let all enjoy the time they have here to develop into the best personality they can be now. If you interfere with that process, sooner or later you will be rejected by them.

To develop into another aspect of life as a multi-dimensional being, you must first know who you are and why you want another person in your life. If your list of reasons for why you want the other person exclusively is long, you are not ready to tie the knot. If your list is short and to the point, we can see you know yourself and are ready to add another person to your life now.

Using the following criteria, add to your list of attributes what you believe another has to offer you, then review it with us:

1. Does your list reflect any area where you cannot function effectively now? For example: Money, sex, education, family.
2. Do you see anything on the list that reflects on you alone? Does it speak to you of needs you now have?
3. Place your name at the top of the list. Does it accurately describe you? If not, why? Write down the areas where you differ from the list.
4. Add a few other items to the list, such as: Name the person you now think is the best or only candidate to meet your needs, then name another, and another. If you have only one you can name now, you are rushing life and need more experience.

Once this world's life is over, you are left alone in your bed or whatever. Who do you think will stand beside you holding your hand then? Work on this thought for a while longer, then let it rest.

Once your life is over, you need not ever come back to Earth, but some will choose to do so, because you are too attached now. We want you to realize Earth is not the only world in which you can develop. Your life here is hindered by people who are not as you are—and by negativity. If the work you do is positive, your work is never seen as bad today by most of the population. This is not the environment for positive outcomes; however, it does present challenges that enlarge and increase your spirit.

When looking at the list you prepared, would you say you had a lot of needs unmet at this time? Do you think another friend or partner should help you with these needs? Do you expect other people to help you? Do you help family and others? If there is a discrepancy in your answers, you need to rethink your needs.

We would like to be around when you pass over to the other side and greet you then, but may not be there. Your friends will be there. Do you have any friends now?

It takes a great deal of patience to be a friend, but it is usually worth the effort. If your friends cannot share their lives with you, you absorb them anyway. If your friends cannot talk about their problems, you understand anyway. You value most the friend who can share and talk over life events, so be as much like that ideal as possible—without dumping problems on others so they will solve your life problems for you.

If you are a friend, you must not ask questions. You must let others know you are interested—but no questions. Once a friend is comfortable, or desperate, then ask questions.

If your life is so comfortable it shows, many will be attracted to you—hoping to steal you away from it. Never let that happen. Encourage others to seek peace. Help them be themselves, but do not let them destroy or disturb the life you worked to build for yourself. Do not be that tolerant!

In the work of the world are many women and men who are unhappy. If you work with such people all day or all night, you may find yourself fearing life. If you do, run water over your body after each workday and eliminate the negativity that clings to you in any way. If your body is covered with negativity, and it can be, you will be unable to shake off the effects of the workplace easily; but if you shower, it washes away negativity easily and immediately.

In many work places showers are provided for cleanliness. It actually serves as a decontamination unit, too. We would like everyone to follow such a procedure. It requires only a few minutes, but can eliminate all static and negative energy produced by the work you do or the people involved in it with you. We suggest you start doing this immediately.

If you think you are the only one desired by another, put your head in an oven and meditate. Everyone wants more than one person to share their life. If your life is centered on only one other person, you will die alone. You need several strong, rooted friendships to carry you through your entire life. If you cannot build relationships, always have to destroy them, your friends will destroy you!

A woman with no women friends is like a cat with no litter or space to claw and strengthen its nails. Women are analyzers and destroyers of reputations, but they of all creatures on Earth love most and deepest. If they cannot enjoy their weaknesses among themselves, they will reach out and scratch out the eyes of other women. It is not a sexist remark, because *The Scribe* is a woman, and we now work mostly with women.

There are women who value only women. These women may prefer women for their friends and/or lovers, but they may not. Sexism is the misconception of one sex about the other, believing they are the only ones who understand their sex. If you normally do not prefer to spend time with your sex, you may be out of sync with your internal clock or biased against your own way of life today. You need to maintain balance. If all your friends are of one sex, you idolize the opposite sex or revile it. Either way, you lose! If you are to progress to the next plane and live as well as possible on this one, you must learn to tolerate and think as others.

When you see people act strange, do you stare at them? It is a normal reaction to disapprove immediately of anything that does not fit your cognitive background, but it must be curbed. React slowly, sit and watch—not stare. Look at the person and determine if something is wrong that you can correct. If there is nothing wrong, let it flow over you and out of your mind.

To ridicule or deride others due to cultural differences is the worst of social behaviors. It strips the other person of dignity. If a situation is not humorous, you should resist laughing at others. If it is humorous, still resist and let the laughter build to a hearty guffaw before releasing it, so everyone will enjoy the power of the energy you then release.

In the old ways of your world a person could rise to the top by simply working hard, but now you prevent all people from rising to the top. Why? We see you often attack anyone showing promise. You attack anyone with superior talents or abilities. You axe anyone who disagrees. Why would you do this when it means the death of a civilization? You do this out of anxiety and despair.

You fear the old ways will return, but they are gone. You believe if you inspire the young to attack the old institutions you will be rejected by them, as you rejected the old, but the young are not after the glory of your age. They want to immediately make a place for themselves in the world. They want a place where they are recognized for being who they are and what they can contribute to the greater whole.

If you cannot ask yourself why you are as you are, you are in bad straits today. If you never ask yourself why, you will never be able to find answers. The only time to be out of sorts with others is when you no longer want them. If you continually act out your own inner turmoil, you will find yourself replacing friends at a rapid rate. You need to slow down your outrage at self and look into the lives of others to see they, too, are upset.

If you believe your problems are greater than all others,
You are selfish!

To be selfish calls forth images of a silly, nasty child waging war with parents, but you are selfish if you ask others to live for you or do your work. You need not worry about your life—it just is. If you ask others to live for you, you will lose your life. If asked to do work and you do it, the outcome belongs to you alone. If you ask another to do your work, they own the outcome—not you. You learned nothing but how to retard your progress. To be unselfish calls forth a picture of tranquility and beauty. May your life be now filled with such scenes.

It takes a tremendous amount of energy to act badly or destroy the work of others, yet it takes so little time to build a work and behave as an adult. If your life is short—and it is, you should save time and act like an adult as soon as possible.

We now move to end this chapter and ask you to follow the exercises provided, but it is important for you to *meditate for an hour first,* if possible.

EXERCISES IN BUILDING RELATIONSHIPS

1. Put your heart on hold and ask for all you can get from life. Once you have it in mind, seek out a friend, then two friends, etc. Only after you have several friends can you seek a lover. If you devote all your time to only one person, you cut your life into too small of fragments. Seek groups first—then single out another to be your lover.
2. If your life is already filled with people, sort out those with whom you are unable to be *you.* Who would you eliminate now? Why? Call each friend and chat, then afterwards ask yourself: Did our conversation sound forced or relaxed? Was I happier after taking the time to visit or saddened by it? Am I now mad at them or me? If the outcome was negative, try once more—before dropping this person.
3. Wait for the next party or reunion with family to ask each one why you are needed at the party. If responses are not

enlightening or positive, you have not contributed much in the past and must begin making your presence known. You have only one tribe on Earth, be a party to it and improve it—*if you despair and want friends.*

4. What you see is not what is there. You must look under the surface if you are to know the other person. Makeup and fashionable attire have been known to lure many a person into a terrible trap. Be sure you know enough before you buy into another's life. Check out their friends and family to know who they are. If they have no friends—run for your life.

5. Don your usual clothes and watch how others look at you. Then put on something quite different from your usual style. How do others react now? You do change with your clothes! Change your wardrobe if you have significantly changed inside, so others will quickly recognize you are different.

6. To put yourself on the auction block and sell yourself to the highest bidder is to be enslaved, yet many a parent wishes a child will marry the wealthiest or most successful person available, instead of *'marrying for love'.* Why? A child ill-married will be their child forever. Your children need to grow up and develop into individuals capable of producing other successful individuals—not remain adolescent in behavior forever, producing immature offspring incapable of living life well.

7. Stack the pages of your life on a table and see if it towers over you or is a jumble now. What would it take to improve the way you live today? Money? Work? Love? Health? You have the capacity to improve all of these, unless you are lying on a bed waiting to die right now.

Before proceeding to the next chapter, complete each exercise.

Chapter Five

The only days you cannot make friends are days when you see no one, so try to visit in the world as often as possible. If you live in an isolated area, make a trip to the outside world—for the world will seldom visit you there. If you are to grow spiritually, it is necessary to seek the outside world.

The inner realm of each person is so deep it cannot be easily attacked by evil nor affected by good. Seek out any and all stimulation in order to affect the deeper side of *you* and help you gain insight into life here. Once the outer world holds no attraction to you, you can begin to seek the inner world.

Some seek the outer world all their lives only to find it vacant of life; however, if you do not seek, you may never find yourself. We do not fear you will become so lost that you never find yourself. It is a rare individual who does not come back to God by the end of a worldly life, but we are here to prevent you from wasting this life and having to come back to rectify something you did now.

In the world of work there are many who are selfish and greedy. If they never learn the error of their thinking, who will still be here? The world gets uglier and uglier the longer you stay around, so let us help you evacuate.

If your only way to navigate is through the stars, you stay up all night. But if the way is clear to you, you can work anytime. We suggest you find your Guides and immediately get to work, so you will be free to work as you please whenever you like.

Never let others know why you are the way you are, and you will never have friends. The only people who can like you are those who have a basic understanding of who you are and how you got there. Others will remain aloof if they cannot label or identify you. If that happened to you, simply begin seeking one person at a time to tell a short life story—please, include no self-pity.

If you only see life through rosy glasses, the world looks pink. However, you need to see it in every light. If the world sometimes goes dark, so what! The colors of the spectrum exist to blend with one another and lighten your skies and world. If you omit one color, it diminishes the rest.

We seek the rainbow!

Some have now rested so long that they have no energy, seeking resting places all along the way and never in a hurry. Will you reach the end of this life with a long way to go? It is not a question of distance, rather the vigor with which you live today.

You must live up to the moment! You need energy even if it is a short burst of time. If spread over a long period of time, you need endurance. Energy and endurance are two sides of the same coin—strength. You need strength, and to maintain strength requires daily work. If your life were to end today, would you have the strength to quickly do it over and ask few questions? You have that opportunity at the end, so be sure you have energy then.

If your life is not within, and you never seek others, you have no life. You are merely a shell. You cannot work if there is nothing within to draw from.

Some people have been known to spend an entire life here on Earth and never develop. Why? They continually said they had no time. They were so busy doing nothing important that they failed to follow through on why they came to Earth. You need to find out why you are here, learn how to help and develop yourself, and then do it. If you cannot learn how to help yourself, you will never develop, because no one else cares if you learn or not.

If your life on Earth was a movie, would you care to see it? We would like you to start seeing yourself as the star in a serial of great length. Would you tune in tomorrow? Would you be so bored by the details that you would drop off to sleep every time it came on—never aware when it was over? Would you want to ask a friend to sit down and watch it with you? Whatever the reason, you have no excuse. You are in charge of your life and must make it meaningful.

To choose to live a meaningful life does not mean it has to fall short of God or you lose your way in the desert. You need only look at the lives of the truly great to see they all relied upon God. You may not approve of what they did, but they did what they believed to be the work of God. It is sometimes obscured by history, but these people are remembered for good.

To do evil in order to be remembered or noticed exists only in today's world—not any other world that previously existed. To ignore the will of God is the self-centered aim of some people today, but it will be erased and forgotten. No one has ever remained on Earth, but some think they will never die—only others. If your evil ways remain unjustified by the time you die, you will be asked to step aside and let another soul return to Earth this time. Others close to ascension are to be permitted to return before evil-doers who intentionally harmed others. We know not where they will be sent then, but it cannot be pleasant.

If the work of 'the devil' (as you like to call evil) is done without remorse, you will notice the world does not punish it. Evil must be punished in some way, and if you do not do it, God will. Punish those who require it and let the rest go. Never harshly punish those who offer themselves up for chastisement, instead go after those who hide their offenses.

When the work of the day does not suit you, others around you are not pleasing either. If you work for a living and see others idling, yet still being paid, you idle. It is the human response and can lead to a life of illness. You must not idle. It will hurt you. If the workplace is not idle but filled with confusion, you will feel sick at work but revive afterwards. It is not wise to work long in confusion, but it often happens when one is busy. To be busy entails a certain degree of organization and development. You will learn more from being busy than being idle. As a result, we favor the busy life.

The life of a recluse is unwise. You may have heard that the hermit develops inwardly, but it is not the same as the person who is out in the world and isolates himself or herself from time-to-time to recount why the world is the way it is. The world is a mystery that needs to be solved, but it does not resolve itself while you sit and stare into space.

If you idly stare, you will soon find yourself out of a job and unable to live well now. If you meditate instead, your work is your best ever and your living increases. Meditation may look like you are doing nothing but staring into space, but you are growing all the time you actively do it.

This is a time of inner turmoil for most people. The godly of each society are appalled at the ungodly ways of others. You must not act like you are superior or you will be forced to act out an act of humility. The humble are wise. If they fail, they have only a short distance to fall. The arrogant are about to see the humble as the only ones on top. Many now are unable to see the top beyond their noses, but the humble continue to plod steadily toward it.

You cannot ask for help and ask for help, and then ask for help again. If you do not have enough time to do a job, ask for help; but if the job is too big for you, reduce the work until it fits you. If you ask for help to do a big job that benefits only you, you will fail. If you ask for help to do a big job that others may share in its benefits, you will succeed.

The only people who know where they are going are almost there. Everyone else continues to figure out what is going on in their lives. To finish all you started, you must first solve the dilemmas of your life and work before seeking others. Once the day is over, you may seek others or go home. If there are people at home, go there. If no one is at home, seek others elsewhere. If there is someone at home, it is not wise to go out and seek others!

The days are ending when you can go about seeking recreation with others who are not after something you have. You must prepare yourself for those who seek sex, power, or excitement at your expense. If you do not, you will lose.

Once you are in trouble, only the past will be of use to you. The worth of the past is to give you experience in handling situations and people. If you lived inwardly and never bothered with outer-world situations or people, how can you know what to do now?

If the idea of a world at war is at odds with *you*, why do you contribute to it? You are if you argue and seek detailed explanations from anyone you differ in opinion. The only one who will ever know peace in the world is one who warred in it. This is not an idle statement, but the truth. You need to learn how to defend yourself verbally and figuratively, but not necessarily physically. If you are quick-witted, you can end your life with nary a scratch, but if you cannot react quickly or with humor, you will be constantly defending yourself figuratively and physically.

When you defend yourself you call forth adrenaline, as well as exercise your inner work. Such exercise always enhances and develops you, thus your glandular system is well suited for argument. If you never argue or shout, the whole system shuts down early in life.

If the work of your body is unlike that of everyone else, you would not know it. Your body is such a mystery to you and everyone else that no one knows for sure what to do when it does not work. Be sure to keep it going, so it does not stop working. The day you introduce the idea you are through living, the body begins extinguishing its flame.

You do not have to do anything!

The only work you ever have to do is live. The rest is the work of your mind. Your mind decides if you will be happy or sad. If the work of the mind is not up to standard, you may be the only one who realizes it, but others will notice your lack of response. You will not be chastised for lacking enthusiasm or intuition, but others will walk away with all the prizes.

The work of the soul is to keep you here long enough to get you to the next plane. If it sounds easy, then think again. This is the reason you are here and now reading this book. You were urged to recite many different mottos, tell tales of valor and glory, and told to be good, but you cannot tell your own story.

You are in need of something. You are never satisfied. You always want something. The reason for this? Your soul thirsts. You have never had any occasion wherein your soul was not involved. You are *you* only when your soul is satisfied.

The only work that can keep the body, mind, and soul together and growing as one is handwork. You must work, so do whatever keeps your hands moving. *The Scribe* is now typing as she works and can keep up easily enough with us, but she also can get her work done, too. You need to do something useful that uses your hands while employing your mind. The soul is then satisfied.

We cannot help you find friends! We are not of your world—and even if we were, teachers would be out of a job if they helped rather than taught. You need to do it yourself.

To discover how many people cannot cope, you need to go into the world and help others. If you cannot cope, you can help others and learn. The work of the world is not as deep as the mind's work, nevertheless it helps to share your thoughts. If you are to fully appreciate the depth of your mind, you need to go into the mind of another.

We are never upset if you read. You also need to speak—and you need to work. If you read a lot, then do manual work to complete your life.

Whatever you do, do it as though you could never do enough of it and soon you will love doing it. If you drag your body through life, acting like everything is tedious and makes you desperately unhappy, you will be upset and unable to succeed. Whatever you do, do it as though your life depends upon its outcome. At some unknown time, it may.

Your life is a series of chores you learned to do. If you initially learned how to work correctly, it takes less and less time to do your chores; but if you idle and pick at work, you will take longer and longer to accomplish whatever.

Some societies encourage minorities to lay back and do nothing. We wonder what the motive is, because you must have one. Why would you want to support another their entire life? Why would you want them to have to return again and again to this life? Who would benefit? What is learned? We suspect it is a power trip for those who think they are better off and can be generous at the expense of another, thus feeling great pride. For some, this becomes a way of life—a way of life that leads to a prison for others or themselves. We abhor the idea of supporting another until they die. You must support the ill, the lame, and the mentally incompetent, but others must be employed.

The only day you need to watch your money is the day you are broke. The rest of the time your money is active and moving, but it cannot grow if there is none. You need money to be social. For example: If you have none, the likelihood of ever marrying diminishes. If your life is not well done and you are empty-handed, you will not enjoy yourself—and you need to enjoy yourself if you are to attract others.

The only day you need to watch your health is when you get sick. The work of the body is to deliver you to all the events of your life; and if it cannot, your life is soon devoid of interest. If your life is not interesting to you, you will not be welcomed by others, either.

Watch the clock to see if your hands are as busy as the clock's hands. If you cannot watch your hands cross and re-cross the page or work at what you are doing, you are not working. Sleeping in the open air is great for the lungs, but your hands cannot work while you sleep. You need to take as much care of your hands as you do your eyes.

The only one who really cares about your work is *you*. If work is tedious, you learn patience. If work is boring, you learn to include us in your life or fill it with some other stimulating work. If your work is not work, you are not busy and will fall into idle ways. If that happens, your mind goes first, your body goes next, and your soul languishes. It is definitely not a good idea to idle.

When you cannot change jobs, you feel as if you are imprisoned; but if you can change and do not, you feel frustrated. Why? Why punish yourself when you can leave a situation? If work is not going well, you may decide to change jobs. Would it help? Would you be better off alone? Would you be better off doing something unlike anything you ever did before? Should you marry? Why worry?

To worry over every detail is not good, but to never worry can lead to a life of illness and bad decisions. Be careful to think through what you want to do, then let your Guides act. If your decision requires a long period of training or instruction, you can begin doing it and find out long before the decision is due whether or not you want to always do it. If you do not know anything about a work or pending decision and its effects on your life, call upon your Guides.

Spiritual Guides are friends of a kind. They will help you maintain an even disposition and fear no one. If you fear *anyone*, you are less than you really are. If you hate anyone, *you* hate! If you are jealous of anyone, you are jealous, and if you do not like to work, you are not well liked.

Your Guides will help you learn to work, and help you choose the job that best reflects who you are, so others can identify you as a kindred spirit. If your life is cluttered with friends of different cultures and backgrounds—not neat and clean, we think you will find it difficult to grow in your own culture; however, it will grasp you by the throat and force you to live. Why would you settle for a one-dimensional life when you can enhance it at any time by including many different people with many different ideas?

The only way to grow is to force *you* to go out and greet others of this life. Once you feel natural greeting people, learn who they are. Some remain *'greeters'* all their lives and never learn a thing about the people they meet. We want you to learn early to greet people—then learn to tolerate all others. If you never talk at length about anything of depth, your life experiences are seldom worth talking about.

In the normal work-a-day world, your life is seldom entered into the fast pace of a race, yet many now think they are in a race. Why? What does your workday look like? Does it in any way resemble a race? We want you to examine the time you are at work. What does it take to get there and back home? A long ride does not become a race, rather a means of transportation if you seek others to enjoy the trip with you rather than travel alone. Once at work, do you run about or walk?

Sit and think—then walk deliberately to each destination. You will never be late again and always be prepared. At lunch you are on your own, but you need never gallop or gulp through meals. That decision is always yours to make. Now where is the race you talk about—a lot?

Everything is within your power!

In the normal world of work are many opportunities to meet people, and you are wise to take advantage of them all. We would not want you to be alone, but seeking the mate of another at work is a dangerous way to live. You must remember that the reason you are there is to work. Once this sinks in and you absorb it, remember you are the only one who cares if you succeed there. If you do something against the norms of the organization, you will not be wanted. Begin to recognize the norm of most organizations is to protect its members, thus a prowling man or woman is of no use to any organization. At work always be cautious of predators—especially the man-eaters.

The work of this chapter was to outline the ways of the world and how it can affect your relationships. We want you to meditate before completing the following exercises and moving to the next chapter.

EXERCISES IN BUILDING RELATIONSHIPS

1. Put your life on hold and let it sit. Does it do anything as it sits? Is it growing more interesting? Do you see anyone asking about it? Are you interested in it?
2. Put your work on hold and let it sit. Does it do you any good? Do you enjoy down time? Do you like to be idle? Is it fun to be idle? Are you nervous? Are you waiting to get back to work or is time hanging idly on your hands?
3. Place your work and life in a bowl and see which is more enjoyable. Do you select work and do it? Do you sit still and smile? Are you able to sit still? Are you able to work and enjoy it? What do you want from work that life has not provided? Sit and stare at the bowl and let it glow and gather energy.
4. Put enough energy into your work to do it well, but save enough to live. If your life is enhanced by work, you feel more like *you* when others know who you are, too. Work on enjoying all you do. Regardless of the degree of difficulty, your work is yours and you are to do it. If you wish to make more of it, do so. No one will complain if you do more than you are asked to do; in fact, most will compliment you.
5. Put your head down and let it droop. Does your body feel energized doing this? No! You must sit erect and let your body know you expect it to produce. Once you know how to control the body, you can control the mind. The only way to be happy is to enjoy your body, and if that takes mind control—then do it!
6. Put your life onto a balance scale and see if it is heavy or light-weight. Lightness of soul is great, but lightness in weight implies you are not working hard. Begin to exceed all the limitations you placed upon yourself. Let out the stops when working and get involved. You may help others, but it is always for your own good.
7. Put your life into action and get a job. Put it out to the world that you like to work. Put your life on the line. Tell people you

can do much. Tell everyone you meet you are busy helping to improve the state of the world. To get a job and keep busy does not mean you have to leave your house; but it does mean you will work—and are working as an integral member of your neighborhood.

The only way to improve your life is to improve all you do. If your life remains clouded and dark, you are not doing what you want to do. If your life is out of sync with all others living around you, please wait until such depression leaves before you move. The first sign of depression often is to see only evil around you, so wait and make sure all is truly evil before you leave a community.

Chapter **Six**

This is not the time to be suddenly out of the world's work. If you are, you must gain credit. The time to be out of work is when the world is doing well, but you are down on your luck. If you are then out of work, another job will present itself quickly—but not now. Now the world's economy is sinking and decaying. It cannot continue to rise above the work of its people.

If you do nothing for years and then suddenly decide to work for others, who will hire you? Not those who manage business. If you show no responsibility or interest in business, no one in business is going to be interested in you. If this is the way your life has been, you need to take the first opportunity to establish yourself as being businesslike. Once you have a job, it is of no use to sit and run it down. Act as if the job is good for you and maybe it will be better than anything you will ever work at again.

In any work there are people who are not easy to get along with, but it is the same whether you work there or somewhere else, so get used to it. The only time to ignore the boss is if the boss is not there. If you could stand and deliver your work, you would not let another downgrade you. Would you? But there are those who will work to destroy the credibility of others and delay their recognition. We will help, if you ask, but you would be better served to watch your boss.

The relationship between a boss and employee is no better or worse than between a servant and master. If you believe you are a slave, you will become surly and niggardly about the amount of work you do; but if you think of yourself as a freeman able to come and go at will, you enjoy the privileges of working at a much faster, efficient pace. Your boss will, of course, appreciate that much more than watching after those dogging their work.

The relationship between you and your boss is the most critical one you have outside of your personal love interest. If you have no savings, you may even find it more important. If upset with your boss, be sure to vent your anger elsewhere. If you wish to get beyond your present position, it is unwise to diminish the effects of your boss's efforts. Many women think a boss is not needed, because they work best at their own pace, but a boss is not there to do the work. The boss on any job is there to see that the work is properly done.

If your work is not done well, you will be offered more than a little encouragement. But if you continue to do work indifferently, expect to be let go or fired. No one wants to be fired, but some bosses know so little about their employees that they do not know who does the work. If that describes you or your boss, define the parameters of the job and get it in writing immediately.

We are never concerned about the job of someone who is efficient, effective, and gets along with the boss, but sometimes we should be. If it is of any interest to you, we have seen people ignored by the top only to be forced into retirement and replaced by people unfit to wait on tables, yet given high positions in management. We do not disparage waiters, but do detest ineffective ways of management to understand its workforce.

In the workplace all know who does what or they should. But if you do not know who you are, who can tell you what you should do? You need to examine the degree of interest you have in your job, then decide if it is better to condition yourself for the long haul or leave now and get another line of work. You will work at one thing or another in life, so why not make it something you like to do?

Once a job is going well, people usually take time to learn the ropes, but the best thing is to learn the ropes first and after a few days dedicate time to learning the job. (If you are unable to decipher the meaning of this, let us try again.) If you take time to meet people and learn the ropes before you get immersed in a job, you will not be cast aside because you do not understand the job. The job is never as deep or difficult as explained by others. If you take time to enter into a relationship with your boss and co-workers right away, you will be there after that job is done. If you do not, your job may be done well and quickly, but still let go at the first cut-back.

When the work of your day is over, do you run home? We hope you do. To stay around the office or workplace long after the day is over encourages you to loaf during the day. You have only enough energy to do one day's good work each day. If you stretch out any day into a longer than usual period, you do not do as good work. For you to work overtime and prosper is analytically not the way to be economically employed. If a company does that very long, it loses money.

When you rush home it implies you are dedicated to your family—which is a redeeming quality if you are less than dedicated to your job. People favor those they picture to be happy and settled. If your home life is chaotic, do not mention it at work! It will harm your image and others will use it against you.

We want you to rush home because someone is waiting for you there. If you have no one, you can rush out and meet others. How else will you learn who you are if always alone? The only way to meet others and not lose yourself is to first be sure you know who you are. It may take years, but your life is yours and requires you to take the time necessary to develop your fullest potential.

If your life has no meaning, it can be disastrous to marry. You need time to learn what matters to you before you ask someone else to share your life. If your life is going nowhere, how do you expect to suddenly aim for the stars simply by marrying or living with someone? You need to be able to identify the major areas of your life and why they are major. If you cannot, you stand in the way of your development. If your life is not done well and you are unhappy, you will not create a good relationship with another—nor can it last. Develop the fullest life possible on Earth; and if you cannot, rest and then take your time.

If the only way you can be happy is to be in a crowd of people, you are not being *you*. The overly fond way of interacting with others some adopt is not realistic. It ignores the fact that people do not act like themselves when away from their base of operation. You would have to isolate each person to determine who affects the rest and makes them react in a manner unlike their usual one, but it can be done.

Work is the only place where you can judge adults' behavior well. If an adult is not liked at work for personality reasons, it is very likely that this one has trouble with people everywhere. Before you can decide if another is without sense, you need to determine why anyone would act like a job is unimportant or not a worry to them. If you can determine why a person acts as they do, you know that person well.

Because the world does not expect you to be *you* in public, worldly ways and behaviors are not the true person or characteristics of the individual. It is expected that you behave as you would anywhere there are others to be considered. You have to be true to your principles, but cannot ignore rules set down by your society or government—unless you wish to pay a penalty.

Are law breakers disliked? To say they are not is misleading to the young and ignorant. The workplace weeds them out first. If the world cannot keep them from injuring the work of others, they will not last long there. You need only look at the door of the employment centers to see who appears most often. There are many who return over and over again all through their lives looking for employment, because they are not wanted. The real reason is they are disliked by others.

When you do your job and do it well, you will have work. If you hate your job, but do it well, you rarely lose jobs. If you hate your work or the people around you and it shows, you will be cast out. The only insurance against unemployment you can devise is to be popular at work *and* do a good job. How can you do good work and be popular? Easy! Do your work, then help others do theirs. If you do not believe it is this easy, try it and see how much in demand you become then.

You can see that if you apply your mind to a job, you may be asked to accept higher and higher levels of responsibility, yet not wish to do more. The way to the top is through increasing levels of responsibility, but you may not see it that way since the politically-correct now work only on what impresses the top rather than contributing to the bottom line. Work—and work hard, but stay on top of your boss's work and that one will like you—a lot.

You were never intended to be politicians, but each of you must be political if you are to successfully navigate the ins-and-outs of the business world today. You are not recognized for good or superior work now, but that will reoccur. *'Business has to be cut back to get rid of old wood'* is what they say, but the remaining wood is so green now it cannot stand straight. If the people left in place have much experience, you could lose many people yet still do a good job. To keep people who only work to impress others results in a loss of financial stability.

You may now see in your line of work others disinterested in you, but if you work hard and ask questions relative to their areas of expertise, you will win their favor. If this sounds like politics—it is, but with a different emphasis. You have to help others get ahead if you are to progress. If those above you remain as is, you cannot move up. To stab them in the back to get ahead will sooner or later result in your being demoted. The back stabbers are always stabbed back.

If your work is done so poorly that you cannot enjoy it, you learn to politicize what you do. Better to instead learn how to do the job right and enjoy it. If you do otherwise, it becomes stressful to even go to work. All the days of your life on Earth are not to be summed up by the work you do, rather it is the effort with which you do it that determines the degree of acceptance you enjoy.

Being accepted by others is the worry of all who are unhappy. Happiness for most is being in the center of admiring and friendly people, but the opposite is not necessarily unhappiness. Worry can end your happiness. To worry over petty things is a waste of time, but the major areas of life do require constant attention to maintain your ideals.

We will now help you identify the petty as opposed to major concerns of your life.

You need to let each day of work settle, then picture it in your mind as if it is sifting through the holes of a colander. If things pass through rapidly, they are small and petty. If the holes clog, small things are rapidly becoming major blockages. Whatever refuses to pass through is of major concern now.

Take time now to sit and adjust your mind's eye until you can fill a colander and let water flow over all your cares. Can you see it? Watch what seemingly floats away. Why worry over what goes away by itself? Watch what happens when the water flows through the holes taking debris with it. Still think it is necessary to worry about what will wash away on its own? The things left in the colander are too big for you to let go of easily, so control them until they are no longer major problems.

The only work in the workplace worrying us is that too many believe they are working when they are not. You often hear people voice their concern that they do nothing worthwhile. Can this be their fault? We wonder if their employers agree.

Would you recommend your job be eliminated? We see it done. Usually, it is hard on the person making the sacrifice, but it often helps the organization. Would you sacrifice a set pace and salary in order to benefit your company? We doubt many would—but why? Why would you not benefit, too, if by eliminating obsolete work you cost the company less money? Most will call out and say it is not appreciated by employers and you would be cast aside without reward. We are concerned that this is true.

When several people are responsible for work and it is not done well, how do you determine who did the poor work? We think you need to restructure your jobs if this is how you arrange them now. We are not of this world, but it is obvious that many managers are not concerned enough about efficient monitoring of their workers. Why be a manager if you do not enjoy such work? Is it because you only want more money?

That is greed! No one takes money for work not done or they intend to do except the greedy.

Greed is the culprit in every place that employs more than one person to run it. If you are the only person in the workplace, would you like to share the profits? No, you want it all. This happens in larger workforces, too. All want the best job, the best office, the biggest company car, the plushest furniture and expense accounts, and no one cares who pays for it. Is that right?

The only way to stop greed is to begin at the top. All who work at the top of an organization hire people to do the work, yet many executives have no inkling of the work their company does—let alone who does it. Where would they place people they hire who are unsuited to do required work? You should know, because they may be after your job now.

When you seek another person to help you do a job, do you tell them to do it or ask? We see women as being prone to tell and men to ask, but it is seldom seen that way by either. Most women say they ask, while men say they tell. You must learn to recognize the facts as they exist in your lives.

A woman who has been busy all her life is happy to be on her own should her mate die, but a woman who has nothing to show for her life will immediately seek another mate. We see you ignore such facts, too. We are not concerned if you argue with us, just be sure you know what is true. The only one to argue is the one who doubts the facts. All others believe as they do and let others believe as they wish.

You argue and disturb one another in order to gain attention. We would prefer that you learn to agree in order to gain attention—then return to your work. If work causes problems within a group of employees, it is the manager's job to straighten it out—not the responsibility of employees. Arguments in the workplace are almost always caused by people working with supervisors who do not manage effectively. It is seldom the fault of the employees themselves.

If you work in a place where all are happy, you soon feel comfortable, too. If you work with sullen, downcast, and disturbed individuals, you will not feel comfortable regardless of how much money and benefits you receive. It is the duty of the workforce to work and management to induce people to get along with one another. Why else have managers?

If your work is not done well, you deserve to be told about it. Do not become incensed and cry foul. Let it go. If you are to improve and do the best work possible, you need to be told. If someone in error chastises you for work you did not do, it is your duty to explain. If they do not believe you or do not wish to hear an explanation, you are already on the negative side of the ledger and need to take time to make some positive deposits to your account or soon be without a job.

You may not totally agree with our assessment of your work, but you know we are aware of work and why you do it. Since that is true, why would we be in error about the rest? It may be that you are in error.

Look at the work you must do,
Does it look like you—really?

If you are suited to your work, you smile and enjoy it. If you hate your work, you look tense, tight-lipped, and generally melancholy. Why inflict such needless pain upon yourself? You deserve the best work. You will love doing some work and hate other work. It is the way of life, but to do what you hate *all* your life is to waste your time. Sometimes you need to work at something unpleasant in order to clear a hurdle before you can jump to the next level—such dedication will not harm you. Your spirit recognizes the difference.

If your only work is for another, such as a woman who lives solely for her children, you will never know the satisfaction they will know from doing their work. You could waste your life and have to return. We do not want that to happen, so we urge all such women and men to seek another way to develop themselves once they are left with no charges at home. However, you do not have to leave your home to find meaningful work.

It is not necessary to venture into business to find gainful employment. Look at what you do and analyze it to determine if the product of your hands is worthy of the time you spend on it. If it is, you are working now. If not, you are merely passing time here. To sell the efforts of your hands is a way of determining if it is worthwhile, but not the only way.

If the only person to understand *you* is You (the Higher Self), you are a success—regardless of what you say. If you do not understand *you*, you are a failure. It is not a big deal to succeed at your work. Indeed, it is a simple matter, but millions overlook it and fail. To fail requires you to return to Earth one more time.

Please look at yourself and analyze exactly why you are, who you are, and why you do what you do. Too simple? Try it! If you succeed, you win and go to the next level—provided your work here is done.

Why would anyone come to Earth? We are all here to work. You came here to complete a particular task that would help your entire being achieve the next plane. If you refuse to follow through, and ignore your work, you will lose the path and refuse your calling, too.

Be sure you are attuned to your Guides so you will hear *the call* when it comes through to you. Your *call* is actually the work you came here to do—not what God asked you to do. It just sounds like that when you hear it.

If work is your life and it is going well, you are thrilled. To share this thrill with another is the greatest of loves; but if there is no one to share it with, do not be upset or depressed. Remember, the life of another means less to you than your own. To say otherwise indicates you are far from knowing who you are.

It is time to begin a few exercises designed to help you gain influence over people and advance in the world of work. If you can do each well, you are a success regardless of the salary you are paid. If you cannot do them well, please work diligently until you succeed. Your work depends upon your ability to be yourself.

EXERCISES IN WORKING TOGETHER

Working out of the way is unwise. Put your plans into action immediately and let others know you are trying to improve—otherwise your efforts may go unnoticed.

1. Place on top of your work a list of things you must do. If the list has more than ten items, you cannot do them all in one day. Eliminate or combine tasks until there are ten or less. After sorting through the list, combine two tasks and work on both.

    If you do the easiest chores first, most of your work will be done before the day gets under way. If you let the hardest work sit at the back of your mind until you finish easier tasks, you will not see it all done until the day is over.

    You do not have to stay late to do your work. That is a game. Only you know how much work you can do. Do it and let others know you can meet their expectations and not disappoint them. Failure to meet others' expectations results in loss of work, but always finishing your tasks on time reverses even the worst employment record.

2. Put your work on hold only if your boss's work is behind. To help others at the same level as you results in their laying back and doing less. If your boss asks, you must help; otherwise, it is held against you if your work is not done—even if it is because you helped a co-worker.

3. If your job is difficult and not well defined, you must ask for simple ways to register the required details so you may be successful. It is details that catch up the most successful. You must know what can be ignored and what has to be done. If you do not, you will eventually fail. It is too difficult to go back and unravel small habits that eventually erupt into major disasters. If small details are not done accurately, it is better to let big things wait.

4. You will be seen as inefficient if your work stacks up—is not moving out. You must develop a pace that keeps your work flowing. To rush—then idle, is not the way to keep work flowing. You have to do it, so work uniformly and act like it

is easy to do. If you succeed, work will be perfect and easy for you. It is all a matter of visualization and organization.

5. When starting on a new job, pitch old work habits into the wastebasket. Otherwise you will continue with the same bad habits that defeated you in the past. If you create new habits before you end old work, you begin fresh and succeed more easily on a new job. Never let one job erode, in order to get a new one. Sooner or later it will cause your career to erupt and explode.

6. To do your best work you need to know *you* and who you plan to be. If you have no plans for the future, how can your present work help you succeed? Work is a means to an end— not the end.

    Visualize placing all your hopes in a glass—then stare at it. Do your hopes look rosy? Blue? Green? Watch the color change as you look at it from different angles. You should see evidence of all colors. Dark hues are undesirable. Light or bright tones are best, if you are going to retire soon. Look for blue green if you need money, and rose if your work is to be successful.

7. Place your work in the same glass as your hopes reside and stare at it. What color or hue do you see? The end result of this visualization is to determine if you are in the right field now. If you are, all your colors will be bright. If not, drab and dark shades fade into brown or black. You need to remove whatever interferes with the color you see until it shines bright. You can do this! You need only meditate several times for more than half an hour each time to change your life. Once you can meditate and visualize like this—your worries are over.

Do not think about these exercises—just do them! You cannot ask others to meditate or visualize for you. It can only be done by you. The work in these exercises prepares you for what you are here to finish on Earth. Your Spiritual Guides are in charge as your boss. Think about it.

Chapter **Seven**

If you think your life is boring—and it is, you should not start over by seeking outside entertainment. Seek the little things that make you feel part of the world around you. Ask a child a question. Seek the answer to a question which always bothered you. Get a lot of reading done. Go into the woods for long walks alone. You get the picture. If time is long and you cannot keep yourself occupied, you are not growing. When growing, the time is short and you are busy.

This is the time to begin new things and act upon them. Once seeds of your success are sown, you can wait for them to sprout, or daily water and feed them so when they appear they have the best possible chance of surviving. Which farmer describes you?

If the work of the fields is not done, what will any of you eat? Many are now leaving the fields to others in order to seek fame and fortune in cities. But why? Fame and fortune can be found anywhere. It is you who determines if you shine or not. Many decide farming is not a worthy pursuit, and others pursue it unworthily. Do what you do—and do it well, and your name will be honored.

If you never seek time to work, instead sit and stare at the wall, you will vegetate. The only growth possible is to live now. If you live and die in the same place and never once move from it, would you be happy? We doubt it much. However, roaming all over the Earth is no guarantee of success either. You must learn to observe the small events and live through the large ones. If you learn from everyone you meet, you know how to live all your life.

We would not like to think anyone actually tries to work evil against others, but it is going on all over your world. Why? Why would you want the life of another when you cannot handle yours? Such egotistical behavior leads to death, war, and destruction. Stop looking at others and begin to examine your life. It is fascinating!

To envy another's possessions is the finest example of sloth you can evoke. Do not sit and stare at work hoping to have it instantly materialize into riches and fame—instead work at it gradually so you can enjoy the process. To sit and stare at another's work and efforts and decide it is not as good as yours is evil and will end in your being held back.

Do not ignore the work of your day, instead put your heart into it and do all you can. Before the end of your life you should be able to account for all of your life's work. If it is even half as well paid as it can be today, it will amount to much.

The only person who can help you is *you*, but if a time comes when *you* cannot do something needed, you will receive outside help. To determine if you qualify for outside help, you must first work and try to do it. If your work fails, or you cannot go further on your own, help will be sent. If no help comes after failure, it is because you can do it yourself or it is not worth your life work.

The only work to do is your own. There are jobs to suit every person on Earth, but few ignore their parents' input and instead seek out what they want you to do. Once an adult, it is your responsibility to seek work best suited to you—not your parents. To accede to the wishes of others once an adult is a way to get ahead, but make sure it accomplishes your goal. If your life is not as clear as it was when you were a child, could it be you were not as clear or free then, either? We see you would rather have freedom now—not clarity. Why?

You need responsibilities to make time fly from birth to death, otherwise you drag through life seeking out work of others to bash. Critics and workers of evil are the same. They laugh or scorn the work of others, but do nothing on their own. We would caution any who scorn or criticize the work of others to watch their lives. We would also warn them to beware of the end. You cannot ignore the laws of God and expect to end up on the way to *'The Promised Land.'*

At the end of this life are times when time drags—because you are idle. You need to be busy. If you sit and stare at walls and never exercise, the body believes it is time to go—and you effectively end your life. You must keep the body active and push it to rise early, otherwise the day is over before the body had enough exercise. To exercise in a gymnasium is a waste of energy. You need to use energy effectively helping others, provided you do not need it for your work. When you go out of your way to help others, it is repaid in other ways. This is of great benefit for your society as a whole.

Wherever you can clearly see the way to the end of your life, you will note your path is not diminished—rather growing—getting wider and brighter. It is not without glistening lights and equally bright, strong emotions. We gain little from ending our time on Earth by helping you stay here. We want you to end your fear of the death process and gain access to knowledge of your past lives so you can finish this endless earthly cycle.

Whatever you do here on Earth is remembered, but not held against you. It is a time of preparation for bigger things to happen above you. If you can thrive on Earth and do much, you can grow anywhere. If you cannot handle the gravity of Earth (we are obviously joking), you will be unable to work on the problems of your entity and thus hold back your soul's progress. Before you mourn this event, realize holding back your soul's progress is not the worst thing that could happen. You could condemn it! If you work evil and never worship God, you may end your soul's existence. It happens!

If you are foolish, you may be asked to repeat a particular episode in your life. If that is the case, you could decide to stay here only a short time. If that is your decision, and you definitely can make it, once here you will suddenly disappear. People, who mourn deaths of the young, need to know they were prepared to leave. If you look into such deaths, you will discover it was not at all a shock to the departed. The only ones shocked are those who knew them not.

We are here to help others recognize the world is not a fearsome place and can be made quite comfortable. You can form relationships for years—and you can end them. It is not the same as life and death. You can be a friend for years and suddenly end it. You can go to your grave in the arms of loved ones or not. It is your decision.

To fear death so much you refuse to form relationships is the most absurd notion we have yet encountered, but it exists. You must let life be the center of your life and let death remain on the outer reaches. Death must never take center stage. It is only a time of passing into another dimension and requires less time and energy than birth.

To begin a new relationship requires a tremendous amount of energy, and you may decide it is not for you. To do this is a mistake if you have few others in your life. It is a wise decision if you have a major personality dominating your life that requires your attention.

Do not seek diversion in love—you will end your love. If you live in the world, you see many people trying to end boredom by entering into liaisons with those who are not free to meet them fully on all levels of life. These affairs are not of any worth if the people involved are not free to merge. These affairs usually end before either person is free to marry. We wonder why they occupy so much of your time.

If your life is so boring it cannot be enlarged by any other means but adding another person, you will find you have many problems with that relationship. It will not run smoothly. You will end it before it is begun, or you will be miserable for years and not have the nerve to end it.

Go for the love of your life, if it is the love of your life. If merely trying to allay pain or suffering the grief of loss, let time heal you—not love. It is of no use to use love of another to help you heal. It delays the process and encourages selfishness. You are to help—not use others. If you use another person to do work on yourself, it never gets done. The other person may honestly try to do your work or help you, but it is your work and cannot be done by anyone else.

The only time to be free of love is when you cannot love. If your life is devoid of love, it shrivels and dies. It does not grow and flourish. You must not let it die, but if it does end, you must move on to another. The time to let a love die is when it has run its full course.

To end a relationship is to end being with the person who causes you to be who you are now. If you are in a bad relationship, this is who you are now and will cause you to become who you will be. If it is a bad relationship for you, it will force you to grow. If it was a relationship that enriched you, losing that person will make you poor. Be sure you know which relationship you have before ending it.

If a relationship is ended by the other, you need to let that one move on and out of your life as easily and quickly as possible. To delay it or inform the other of your desire to continue at any cost is a waste of your time and energy. Instead, go for the goal of your life and see how much more distance you can gain now.

The pain of ending relationships is overemphasized in your culture. It is seldom as sorrow-filled as portrayed. You move, you grow, you develop—which results in endings. So what? It also results in new beginnings! Most are more interested in beginnings than endings anyway, so let not your heart be worried over the way to end a relationship. If it is time, it will end of its own weight.

The only sorrow to be taken seriously is the worry of being the one to end a relationship before the other person is ready. This is a tragedy for one—not the other, and requires tact. You must not let your fears and feelings of guilt outweigh the reason for dropping this person. You have to live in the vacuum created by the loss of this relationship, which will hurt you as well as the other until time erases all ties.

The only sorrow worse than telling someone you do not wish to continue to be their friend is to hear that you betrayed a friend. This is truly a mortal sin, one which can be heard all over the universe. You shall never be forgiven for intentionally hurting one who trusts you. If you hurt another intentionally and do not explore ways to reduce their pain, you will one day experience the same degree of torture. If the pain is slight, you will experience only a slight ache. If you were treacherous and deceitful, you can expect the same in return.

We would love to talk about all the ways of treachery, but what would you learn from it? You are all so silly when it comes to love. You love first one—then another. You seldom sink everything you have into a relationship, so why worry if the other does the same? You think you can like someone and they in turn will love you. It does not work that way. If you love, you may be loved in return; but if you merely like another, it is unlikely you will receive anything deeper in return.

Whatever you do, do it as though it were the only time you will ever do it—which includes love. To love half-heartedly is to waste your time. To love disinterestedly is not love at all, it is ego gratification and will do harm. To love as though you could never love again will result in the harmony of the ages meeting within you.

When you love and lose, you learn. If you play at love and lose, you say you learn not to love. You learn to play and play and play, but not how to love someone. To spend a life never really loving anyone is the saddest of all wastes of lives. To love at least once is required to pass to the next plane. You cannot learn to tolerate others if you have never loved anyone but yourself.

This is not the time or place to rearrange your life, but you must begin if stuck in your present life. Once you know who you are and why you are, you can love others. But to love, you must know who it is you want and why. For you to fall in love and stay in love, you need time to become familiar with the other. If you rush into marriage, you will often be sore with each other before the honeymoon is over.

Why risk killing a beautiful friendship?

Putting others beyond your reach is not wise. If you love, it means you understand the other. How can you understand someone you are in awe of and cannot reach? You need to develop your esteem so you live a larger life—not marry someone in order to gain one.

Some are aware of the work going on in this world now, but remain aloof to it. If you are to reach the next plane, you need to understand this world. It is a class of work that requires your total involvement. If you never participate, you will never be able to explain why you were here.

This is the goal of the next plane: to explain why you did what you did while here. If you cannot understand why you are here, you need to look into the mirror of your soul. To do this, simply meditate. Your Spiritual Guides can speak and solve all your problems, but you have to clear your mind in order to hear them, then you have to follow through and do what is required.

If your life is in a muddle, you cannot help anyone else. It is egoistic to believe you can. Once your life is on the right path, you can begin to help others sort out facts, but help comes only from God. You need to fully understand you are only human—not God-like or even godly.

What you never see is the work going on all around you—to help you. If you could, you would understand why no one else on Earth has the power to help others. It requires far more than humans can possibly understand. We always welcome well-intentioned people who try to help others sort through their lives in order to settle on what is most pressing to them, but only God can clear a mind of pain and sorrow.

The only time to be worried is if your time is short and you have nothing on the way to being completed. If you die at a time when you are half-done, you will be returned and asked to complete this life's goals—plus what you need to do that life. It gets harder and harder to free yourself of Earth, so get busy now.

To begin to understand the nature of relationships on Earth compared to those on other planes will be discussed in the next chapter. You need to thoroughly ground yourself before you begin that work, so we prepared a list of problems and exercises that hinge upon the work you are doing now in your life. If you cannot begin this work immediately, leave the next chapter untouched until later and skip to Chapter Nine.

EXERCISES IN WORKING INTO
AND OUT OF RELATIONSHIPS

1. Put your hands on the floor and walk like a camel. Do you feel strange doing it? You look and act different when not standing erect—even your voice changes. You must stand up to be *you*. If you bend over backwards and stick out your stomach, you look like a pushover. Stand, sit, and walk erect. If you never bend over backwards or clomp about like an animal, most people will respond to you with respect.

2. Place your feet and legs together. Do you see anything strange in doing this? We want you to stand tall with your feet together—not slumping to one side or the other. Notice how many people slump one way or the other. If you see others standing with their feet together, you can assume they read this book, too. No one else will notice it but you. Go to that person and ask if they are doing any spiritual work—worded any way you like, but ask. It is no big deal if they say *"no."* You will have started a conversation with a stranger on an interesting and uplifting note—which is how to make friends.

3. If your car needs a front-end alignment, do you place ads in the paper? No, you read ads instead. You advertise when you have something to sell—not buy. People who advertise themselves as dates are not interested in buying—only selling, so avoid them. Never put faith in blind ads. You do need to sell yourself, but buying air time is unwise. Put yourself in the buyer's place. *'Why would I want anything others don't want? Why would I want an old model when a new one is nearby?'* Reach the point where you know why you desire someone who advertises—then do it, too. (You will never reach that point.) Put on a hat and go to

the corner store and talk. It is more likely you will meet a mate there than through an advertisement.

4. Pull out old magazines and look at the pictures. Find scenes of people gathered in a family setting or out on a date. Paste them on a large poster board—adding similar ones until you have a collage of photos of relationships in all stages of development. Then hang your collage near your bed and look at it before going to bed and when you wake up. As you visualize, it will come to pass for you, too.

5. To end a relationship, first demand the attention of the other party. Once you have the attention of whomever you wish to discharge from your life, act calmly, taking no time to discuss the reasons, and say, *"I'm leaving and will not be back."* Then go and never return. It is truly that simple.

6. To end a relationship when it is going through a difficult period is to accept you failed. You must not let it end until you know why it failed. If you do not know why, it will happen again and again. Do the work and find out the reason!

7. You need only a pencil, paper, and time to figure out one's chances of living happily together. Ask: Are you happy? Do you want children? Do you have enough money to live on now? Do you want more? Do you want to go to school or college? Do you want your children to go? What would you do if you could be anyone you wanted to be? What do you think of God? Why are you here? What is wrong with the world? Enough questions to last a long time, but ask them all before you marry. If you do not, you will discover the answers and may not like what you find—but too late. Ask before committing yourself to a relationship. It is easier—and the marriage will last longer.

No one would want to marry a man or woman just to be married. Would they? You are the best judge of that. If you said *"yes,"* start work immediately on your personality. You need help to determine why you would want to marry just to marry. If a life crisis is without end, you will never be able to marry. You would need to counsel others to hear *every* rationalization—but you get the picture.

To get a job, never sit and simply work on a list of your credentials. List all your traits of character as well—and stand behind them. Your character is what is tested in a relationship—not your work. You can list several people as references, but make sure at least one actually knows you.

This is the end of our discussion on relationships as they apply to marriage. We will now enter into the necessary relationships that also exist between people *and* others who command our respect.

Chapter Eight

The only time to exist without God is if you believe you are God. How is that possible? We will help you give up the belief you are not in a world of your making, so you can understand what relationships are to *you*—not to anyone else.

Once you can understand that the world is not wrong, rather the people who control it, you will be able to stop the madness. If you were in charge now, how would you change it? Would you place taxes on all who work in order to support those who do not? Would you expect the old to help? Would you expect the young to be belligerent, evil, and demanding respect for merely being young? Would you ask others to do your work? Would you expect everyone's work to contribute to your life? These are the ways of the present world. Why would your world be any different if you were to lead?

We want people here to change the world into a place suitable for the angelic realm—not earthly pastimes where you cannot tell the wealthy from the poor. We want you to know the difference between a lifetime of poverty and wealth. We want you to decide immediately if your work is good or evil. You need to decide all of these things yourself!

If your world is not of your making, you would try to change it to how you see it, but few do anything. You sit or talk about the wild and wily ways of others, but never stop them. You let youth of your societies rule as though they knew much. You act as if you are the only one who cares. Why?

If your life is to run smoothly, you need to know why you are the way you are. If your world is to run smoothly, you need to be there to make it happen. If you do not like your work, you must change it until it suits you.

These are the basics—you must do them first!

In a relationship the only one to be *you* is you. If you renege and change into another, and another, and another personality in order to please those you meet along the way, you will soon be lost. If you remain the same and never change, your life will stagnate and grow boring, and you might decide you are stupid.

It is easy to be alive. All you have to do is eat, drink, and sleep. You do not have to do anything else. Some people do only this for their entire lives, but who wants their lives? It is easy to be interesting, just talk to others and learn from them. Once you know who you are and why you exist, tell others. It is a lifetime quest.

We are not of this world or even of Earth, but we can see you clearly do not realize Earth is not the only planet where people exist. You are so self-centered and egotistical you believe you are the only ones, but you are not. We would be the last ones here if you were. You are not the only ones to face extinction, but the first who caused it yourselves. This makes you the most stupid of all God's creations!

As teachers of the higher realms, we are not here to ask you to straighten up your grades or act like mature beings. We are here to act. If you do not add to your life, it will disappear. You have nothing else to save. You can exist like this while here, but on another plane you will be chastised for lack of concentration, plus any destruction you committed while on Earth.

To begin to understand why we were sent, you need to decide if you believe in God. If you do not understand that God is—you cannot understand any of this. You will continue to be cursed with ignorance and disbelief until you shed it. No one else can help you believe in God.

To believe in God is easy. It takes much effort and energy to deny God is, but you can do it. We are not here to waste time (as you see it) or energy if you do not have enough sense to begin to understand why you exist. The others present are of no interest to you, either, if you cannot accept us.

To believe in God takes nothing from you, but adds to *you*. If you believe, *we will help you seek the way*, but will not bother to answer your questions if you are insincere. Why should we? We are not God. We do not care if you pass or fail. We are merely teachers of the higher realms.

To believe in God is not the only belief you must hold. You have to believe you exist. If you do not grasp this simple idea, you cannot believe you have power. If you do not have power, you are unable to change the world. The world is not of Earth, it is created from the thoughts of men, women, and children. You have let it become disturbed and placed in a lost orbit, but order can be restored. Earth cannot be restored, but your world can be saved!

You need to keep your aim high so it is not too far off the mark. You also need to keep up with your life. If you fall behind trying to restore the world, your life is lost for nothing, because then the world does not exist. The world is the result of your combined efforts to act as one. You need to cooperate, but it cannot be at the cost of your life.

If your life is dull, listless—bores even you, why would anyone else want to share it with you? You must believe in *you*! If you do not, we cannot accept as fact that you want to believe in God. If God was not the most powerful force in your life, who would you have instead? We see you never go beyond the elementary…

This chapter deals with the relationship between you and others of your species. It does not matter if they are romantically attached to you or not. You are the only one who cares if you have a life, so begin seeking experiences and people who will enhance you. Do not live in a tunnel and run out the other end when prodded by the light. Get into life. Live as a personality of the highest order. Anything less is not living for *you*.

We would expect you to tell others about your life but not boast. You cannot boast about what you know nothing. Your life is a mystery as long as you live it. Once you pass over, this life becomes a story enjoyed or agonized over time and time again.

The choice is now yours!

We want you to begin taking care of your life responsibilities. If you let them grow and never accept that this is your life, you will leave this life a bitter and unhappy person. If you accept that your life is your life, all is happy. Once you recognize you are not a special entity being given rare privileges, you can expect to enjoy peace of mind and the comfort of old age. You must work. You must be *you*—and you must get along with others.

If your life is not as complete as it would be if you had another person living with you, you may exchange one aspect of your personality to gain another person, but be sure you want to give up a part of you here. It is not enough to desire companionship—you must be able to share everything. If you do not like to share, how would you find life pleasant within a marriage? The only work of this world that causes *you* trouble is the work of your life here.

You do not care if your father and mother part. You do not care if your sister or brother dies. You do not care if someone else is terminally ill. You care only if it interferes with the free flow of your life. That is the adolescent mind that resides within all people. Adults can empathize and agonize with others. No one else can live for you or be mature for you. You alone must grow, plan, and work to create an adult of great stature. We will help you or not to do your work—it is your choice.

If your life is short and you have much work left undone, we suggest you live it up and let go of the past. Living it up does not mean you waste time or ignore others. It means you live up to your potential as much as possible. We will help you.

If your life is not short now, and you expect to be on Earth for many more years, act as if you will not be here very long. This is how to get the most life out of your years. To act otherwise encourages laziness. You must never let yourself become lazy. Not that it is evil, but because you need time to be *you*. If you spend everything you have lazing about and ignoring your life here, one day you will end up having to return to Earth. We do not want you to return!

Whatever the day, it is here for you. You do not need to spend time on anyone else. It is your decision to give your life away to others. So if it is your way of being you, be happy. Do not regret having helped others. You need them to help you discover who you are and why you are, but you do not need another to be *you*. This enigma (to you only) is so easy for us to see, we wonder why you are so dense.

To enjoy the life of women in your society is to say you want it all. *We would correct that to read:* We want to be all we can be! That is the correct way to read it. If you want it all, you will never enjoy what you have.

You need to enjoy you,
You need to be You,
You need YOU!

Whatever work you do on Earth is not worth much. It may appear to be more important than another's life, but it is not. It is a means to an end—YOU. You are not to sit and angle for hours trying to out-fish another. You are to fish for yourself.

If you sit and finagle with financial schemes that destroy the livelihood of others, you will pay for it. We see you think wealth is the sign of a life well-lived, without considering how it is arrived at by the individuals involved. You will have wealth.

You all will know peace, but it takes time. If peace is to be understood, you must first know war. It takes a warrior to establish lasting peace. Those who do not fight for another are unaware of the relief at the end of such war, because it is not their fight. If you fight for a cause or belief, your life is enhanced to such a great degree you may seek out another cause or belief to champion—and another. We suggest you learn all you need from one war and leave the next to others.

It is not the time to dwell on war, but we want to acknowledge the need for dispute and disregard for peace if times are not good. If you accept peace at any cost, you will pay dearly for it. If you accept no peace, you will lose your life. It is a wise person who accepts peace after a time of strife, when it becomes apparent he or she cannot win. It is the fool who continues to struggle long after all others have given up.

We know it exists in your societies, but cannot begin to understand why anyone would take on your life in order to have your riches. We see many envy and behave in a jealous manner toward others who have worked hard to achieve fame and fortune. Why? You could do the same. It is a choice of one life over another—and you chose your life. It is not the other person who chose your life—it was you who did it. If you ignore this basic principle and continue to irk us with this pettiness and ignorance of the facts of life, you will be gradually dismissed from class.

We cannot condone the bad behavior of any student who may represent an entire class. If your behavior is not up to the standard of others, you cannot be given their privileges or extended credentials. We are not here to push you through the process of enlightenment or help you be *you*—that is your problem and must be worked out by you alone.

Before this day is done, you need to ask if anyone else sees things as you do. If no one does, it does not mean you are wrong. If everyone agrees with you—and that could happen, you may still be on the wrong track. Look at this world, who do you think made it this way?

When the work of a day is done, your life begins. You need work to ground and fortify you for the trials and errors of your inner work. If the inner self is less strong than the physical body, you will notice fatigue. If the outer body is less strong than the spirit within, the body does not complain of fatigue. This is true!

Whatever you do, do it well and do it fast. If you could hurry your life, you would. It is so much better above that we share a few items of interest so you may know why you should not linger here. It is not time to begin advanced studies of the upper planes, but it will come in time. Your time here is now. We will help you understand the need for speed by explaining the time frame here as opposed to the time structure everywhere else in the universe.

If your life is not what you want, and many of you treat it as if it is not, we would never bother to explain anything; however, many of you are here to learn. The lesson of Earth is: You are not the only one. You are among millions of light beings advancing toward the core of existence known as God. If you accept this, you are half way to your goal. Any other response is registered as a negative reply and indicates you have to work on Earth longer.

In the universal scheme of things you are the only one to begin a journey, but all will end. *It is not a misprint.* You are to end as one. If you explain this to a child you will notice the intent is not to frighten. If you explain it to an adult, the intent is to educate and elucidate without intimidating that person. If you never seek to learn, you fear. Is this how an adult of the world should act?

Whatever you do now is the result of past choices made by you. If you chose to come to Earth (you did), and you asked for your parents (you did), and you asked for your body (you did), why would you now blame God? It is a fool's world that believes God would in any way harm or hurt those who believe. It is a fool's way to blame others—even God, for what he or she chose to do. We care not for fools or their friends, but try to please all who ask for help regardless of their past.

A fool is never seen as a fool. Only those who cross over the lines of your society are seen as foolish, but many who obey all laws and seek out respect are fools. You may not think they are, but their attacks on higher beings of this universe mark them for distinct disfavor. You would be wise to set your eyes on a goal achievable by you that does not entail belief in another person. If that other person is proven to be a fool, you could be drawn into the same vortex.

Once a soul is destroyed, a vortex is created that can and does pull into it others of like mind who have not anchored their lives on rocks of faith. To be sure your mind is not idly wandering about when such a soul goes down, so meditate on YOU. The day a soul dies in agony is not the same as the end of the world, but it is the end of that soul's world. You will be threatened by death in this world, but it is nothing compared to the eternal damnation of your being. It is nothing!

To suggest some people create evil and then go forward is to blasphemy God. No one who creates evil is advanced—ever! You are here to learn, so you make mistakes. If you do not care for others and act accordingly, you hurt your life, but not anyone else. This is the nature of this world.

To learn through trial and error is most effective; but if you set out to enter a life of sin and produce concrete works of evil, such as Hitler in World War II, you will know your life cannot continue on Earth or anywhere else. That soul is eternally banned from further growth and will continue to exist in a tortured life of evil visited upon it at every turn in the path until it learns the meaning of the pain and suffering it inflicted. In the case of Hitler, you may expect it will last forever.

To explore the realm of nature to determine if animals are evil, you need to explore the realm of your individual self to determine if you are evil. If your search permits you to explain yourself, you may be allowed to explore others—even animals and other beings present on Earth, but you are the first course. You may not skip *you* and go to the second course.

If your courses are mixed and inadequately represent your life on Earth, it reflects bad guidance. If that is the case, you will be given help to recognize your ways are not influenced by anyone greater than who *you* are. If your Spiritual Guides are greater than *you*, why would they ask to help you? They are above *you* and seek out greater responsibilities. These Guides are far more knowledgeable about *you* than we are, but you are the only one to become *you*. If your knowledge of You is superior—and it should be, you will call upon your Guides only when you need help—not to live as is, but to grow.

Some of you are advancing at great speed into the work of the next plane in order to help at the end of work here, but you need to rely less and less upon your Guides if you are to be ready to move up into the angelic realms. Once the work of your Spiritual Guides is completed—and it can be, you will be asked to lend assistance. You will be asked to push forward the purpose of your life and explore inner life, but not before you are ready.

For you to seek help from the upper planes before you are ready will result in demotion. You cannot expect the higher realms to help those who refuse the help offered here, which is stupid (besides being arrogant). You are to seek your Spirit Guides here on Earth until such time as you are permitted to seek higher help—but not before.

Many well-meaning people are directing those of lesser ability and will to directly ask angels to help them accomplish mundane chores here on Earth. This is beyond the belief of those who have worked here and still help. You are bypassing aid given by those still growing toward the light, as you may be, but far more advanced.

We will give you a few ways to contact your Spiritual Guides here. If you are uncomfortable doing any of these exercises, we suggest you devise one of your own. You may not alibi out of never calling your Guides. We seek only to establish a link between you and your higher self, which comes from inner growth—not outer show. Begin now to read and study. If your life is not enhanced, *then* let your life go and ignore our advice. We know you will never do that!

The following exercises are not the only ways to contact your Spiritual Guides, but very reliable—especially for beginners. Please welcome all who work for You. Respect them as you would anyone with superior knowledge of the workings of *you* and this world. If you need further help, Guides are authorized to call all to your assistance—BUT it is their call! Neglecting to follow rules is not a sin, but to willfully accede to your life and step on others to do so is a sin.

Put your life on hold for a few more minutes. Read through the following list first, then return to the easiest exercise for you to accept and use readily. It will be difficult for some to erase the words of ill-meaning people who attempt to frighten the insecure or ignorant into believing some other being can take over your soul during prayer and meditation. Why would anyone believe such nonsense? We do not know, but it is easy to become confused in a world of false prophets. Be true to You and do what is best for *you!*

EXERCISES IN CONTACTING
YOUR SPIRITUAL GUIDES

1. Focus your vision in the center of your mind by closing your eyes and seeking the space between your eyes know as *'the third eye'*. Concentrate. Think of nothing! If something appears, let it intensify and grow and blossom into life. Be not afraid of the work of your mind. Let it imagine it can be anything and enjoy your creativity. Paint the scene in your mind and forget to erase it.

2. Seek your *'third eye'* and sit still for several moments. Do you hear anything? Do you see anyone? Are you relaxed? Concentrate on the depth and precision of your mind, but do not fasten your attention on anything. Let thoughts flow. This is meditation. Once your meditative state is deep enough, your Spiritual Guides can contact you; you will be able to hear them.

3. Put one hand in a basin of warm water. Let the heat enter your pores and advance upward to your elbow and shoulder areas, then place the other hand into the basin and warm your other arm. When both hands are warm, the mind is free of constricting thoughts. You need only let your mind wander. If the water grows cold without feeling any movement within, dry your hands and try again another day. Guides like warmth.

4. Place a candle in the center of a table with a stone on either side of it for balance. Once this little altar is erected, notice it has become a spot of serenity. Place your mind at ease and stare at the candle flame. You are not relaxed when you see the flame constrict and contract. When you see the flame grow, you are. Watch the flame to see if its movement produces an image. If it does, ask for your Guides, otherwise sit still and meditate

on NOW. In time your Guides will come to you during this practice.

5. Place your feet on a chair or cushion elevated above your hips. Relax and let the blood flow back into your pelvis. If you carry much tension in this area, you will feel more at ease if you lie back. While the blood flows into your pelvis, ease up on work of the day and let your mind free itself of worry. Let tension flow through your chest and out the top of your head. This reversal of the flow awakens the crown chakra where energy enters. To reawaken a chakra, simply rest and remove tension from that area. No other accoutrements are required. Stones are helpful if you lack grounding and are too spacey, otherwise you need nothing. Relax and enjoy the life within you. Your Guides may be there then, too.

6. Set your mind to think about a clock. Let the clock's hands slow until it stops. If you can stop time, you are there! You have no problems. We want you to completely stop time. If your life is out of control, listen to the clock. If your life is dull and boring, speed up the clock until your heart feels a difference, then let it stop. Your life is measured by your interior clock, not by time set by others—believe it or not! Once the clock stops, begin breathing deeply, exhaling the negative aspects of your life. Count your breaths and end the count at whatever number suits you. In time you will need only to count to four to realize your life is your life—until then, count as far as you wish.

7. Place the time of day on an interior wall and make an entry into a mental diary. If your day was exhilarating, place a glowing comment now. If your day was a disappointment, sigh. If your sighs are louder and longer than your comments, you quickly need help from your Guides. By simply asking aloud for help, we will help you contact them, but first establish why you are unhappy and what you need to be the best ever this life—then your Guides can easily work with you.

8. In the furthermost reaches of your mind visualize a chair and lamp. Regardless of where you are, enter that area whenever your work is done. Sit in that chair, turn on the lamp, and look at your work. Shut out the world. Sit and stare at the lamp

without seeing it. Do you fear anything? If you do, look into the light. Do you know anything? If you do not, read the book now laying on a table beside the chair. You are reading your life. What does it say? Pause your heart by slowly saying: *"I am able to concentrate. I am able to seek all I know. I am me."* In time this affirmation will enable you to seek your Guides, but be sure you need them first.

It is obvious you cannot contact your Spiritual Guides if you cannot calm yourself enough to hear them. If you cannot meditate or pray, your life cannot be restored to its original path. It is your decision whether or not you will restore your life to what it can be. No one else cares whether you do it or not. If you do not care, please refrain from complaining to those who do. It is never appreciated.

We end this chapter with one admonition: Do not eat and then meditate, unless you plan to seek total rest. The heart has much blood to pump. If it does not have a chance to restore itself, your life here is shortened. Take care to never upset the body holding your spirit and Spirit will heal the body when needed.

Chapter Nine

The only way to be without pain and suffering is to inflict none upon others—even then it may be a habit you established long before you awakened to Spirit. To end it, you must acknowledge the relationship between pain and your life.

You may have had a lot of trouble this life, but so have all others you know. It is selfish and self-centered to believe you alone have problems. You will discover that all who live enhanced their lives through problem solving. You need only check into any library and check out biographies. The writing of any book is a labor of great worth, but to write of another's life is the most difficult story to write, because you have to face their problems while living through your own.

To admire others is not the best way to study them. You need to know their good points, but also need to know why they were the way they were—which seldom comes from being raised in a calm, serene setting. Most admirable people lived with chaos most of their lives, which enabled them to sort through the dross and discover gold. You, too, can be a great and noble person, but it takes a lifetime to know if you are. Seek the best and the best will be yours.

To seek another human for emulation and duplication of their goals is to waste your life. Decide early in life if this is to be a time of growth or stagnation. If you are here to grow, you need to fully develop without interference from adults with less than admirable characters. If you are here to stagnate—and who is, then seek the poor of heart and soul and congregate on the corners of your town and run down all who are of worth. A life of idleness leads a soul to return and return to this Earth.

Whatever your life's goal, it cannot be the same as anyone else's. That is not to say you will not have similar aspirations to be great, but you cannot all be the same since you are all different. Whatever you do, do it all. Do not sit and idle. Seek action and betray no one.

Where you fail is in not doing *your* work. All of their lives people seek goals, so be sure to seek your own. To help others reach their goals is an end in itself, but to help others and ignore your goal results in you returning to Earth!

Whether or not your life this time is easy or hard, you chose it—it is your life. To believe God distinguishes between souls and metes out hard lives to evil-doers is placing God beneath you. It is not the role of the judge to serve the sentence. God loves from within and acts upon you as you live a life of strife or happiness.

God is not a judge

You judge everyone you meet with equality—either consistently harsh or lenient. Which describes you? If your life is judged harshly, you may be aware it is not as great as if judged leniently, but the lessons are more deeply learned. Whichever you choose, we will support you to this end.

What you need to do when you fear someone is to remove that person's warrior armor and don it. You will see it has chinks that permit the entrance of many death stings, but the warrior knows how to protect against such attacks. Learn to protect yourself in tight places—physically and mentally, and spiritual forces will rescue you.

If your life is no more ready than a fireman without a hose or ladder to put out an eventual blaze, how can you expect to be saved? You must be in charge! You have to know what you can and cannot do. If your life is a total shambles, take it all in and spill it out. Do not regurgitate your life story, just spit out the bile. Once the story of your life is palpable, you can enter your partner's life—but not before.

You are not a trained therapist. Even if you are a therapist, you are not trained to investigate *your* mind. It takes a person of great intellect to detect the problems of the mind, and it can take years to determine how one mind works—and that mind works unlike any other mind. So where do mindful people find help?

Form your inner sources

Your inner life is varied and deep with nothing to offer the outsider. It cannot be deciphered by anyone but you and is not the work of anyone else! It consists of all you are and all you want to be and cannot be manipulated. You are the only one who can change you. To believe others can control your mind or take over your mind is a sad reflection on you. That anyone would say such things to another is unpardonable. It reflects their poor impression of you.

Do not sit and idle away hours doing nothing. If you do, your imagination can worry you to death. It is not necessary to die. You merely stop living. You cannot live in a body that does not function, and you cannot think with an idle mind.

You need to constantly exercise

You must exercise whether or not you like to do it, so we suggest you quickly learn to enjoy it early in life. People who are happy have a strong life force. Your life force is not the only means to provide energy, but it is within you and controlled entirely by *you*. No need to call angels or others from higher realms if you live with care and prepare while here.

To never feed and let the body evaporate results in physical death— but what happens to the mind? Your mind is every bit as active as your body and requires its own source of food and inspiration. Read to enrich the mind, think to use what you have, and exercise it. Believe—and reap the rewards! It is not hard to believe once you read with interest and prove all you need to know.

Whatever you do, you do it for *you*—not for anyone else. To believe you do things for others is a fallacy. To believe others think about you a lot is also a fallacy. All anyone can expect from another is that they will be considerate. You need to understand that basic tenet of human behavior before you can be free from hurt and despair.

When you seek aid and no one wants to help, it is best to do the work yourself or give it up. If it means much to your soul, it will be done with help from higher realms. If ultimately it is of little use, no one will come to your aid.

Whatever you do, you do it first within *you*. You learn what can go wrong before you actually do it. Once you understand this concept, you can use it to develop a complete line of thinking designed to produce a life of ease and reduce stress.

You need never worry!

Do not fear! You can be *you* and still be well-liked. In fact, you have to be *you* before you can learn to rest this life.

Now that this chapter has been reviewed and we can see it, the work flows. Once the work flows, it takes little time to do it. To start working before a task is thought through results in loss of time.

Take all the time you need to develop a theory. It will shorten the time it takes to prove it. If a theory is from the upper realms, you never need time to develop it. It comes totally thought through. Your life is totally thought through before you arrive on Earth, but many refuse to touch back and see what you are meant to do. You get lost in the shuffle and seek no one's help—not even your own.

What you need to develop a positive outlook is to first develop a positive outcome. You will never feel confident if the project is not thoroughly understood—or not apparent to you that it will succeed. You must not proceed with anything that cannot be visualized. If you do, you run a great risk of failure. The only way to be *you* is to visualize who you are. If you cannot do this, may we suggest you sit down at the end of this chapter and learn to visualize now?

To live in a world of great beauty and never see it is blindness that surpasses sightlessness. To be deaf to the song of the Earth is to be dead within. To sense nothing around you when all others are moved is an indication you are callous. To sense much while others remain motionless is not necessarily an indication they feel nothing, rather you are more sensitive.

A goal of the artist is to remain sensitive all your life. You need pain to know much. You need help to seek out the growth of the mighty, but you need not die.

The work of the world is to encourage you to be *you*, regardless of the delay or suffering along the way. If you take your life, you delay suffering. We will not permit you to advance, if you take shortcuts—and suicide is a shortcut out of this life.

If you take another's life, you will not necessarily be incarcerated on Earth, but you will be told and expected to pay for it when you attempt to cross over to the other side. You cannot escape punishment. It awaits you, so we suggest you own up to it while here—and be ready to cross over at death. To wait until the end does not help you advance.

Your time on Earth is a long relationship between you and the life force within you. If you never feared anything, fear your life force is not strong enough to take you all the way to the end of the life you mapped out for yourself. If your life force dwindles and cannot sustain you, how can you live? We will let you starve the body, but never the soul. You share whatever power the body has with your mind, but the soul is fed directly by Spirit.

You never starve *you*—you starve your body. You never feed your body, you feed your mind. If you fed your body, you would eat only the most nourishing materials—and seldom eat even that. Instead, you eat to serve your mind. The mind determines what it wants and you feed it. If you change your mind, your body responds. If you try to change *you* by changing your body, the body quickly reverts to how it was before the change.

If your body is in control, why would you want to be a human being? You would enjoy material being then and not be aware of others. You would be a mindless blob. To seek knowledge about the body is very wise, but it seldom takes a wise man to understand the body is not what it appears to be.

The body is not at all like You. It does not look at all like YOU! Your body is a flesh and blood personification of the genetic trace of past generations and is reflective of the attitudes of your society. If you see beauty in your form, it is because your society taught you to believe that way. If you believe you are strange or grotesque, you have to learn to live within your society or evade it. Do not mutilate your body to please others. It causes you to fear deep within you that no one will accept you as you are.

Put your life on hold if you want to learn how to live. If you rush about and cause confusion, you cannot learn much. Sometimes it is necessary to rush, but it seldom is the result of planning. Please be prepared for unnecessary work and avoid it, but do not put off work that must be done.

You cannot hold back anyone else! You can only hold yourself back. If the other in your life wishes to proceed down the aisle with another, you should remain still. If the other forces you to follow, you should resist. We seldom see anyone forced to do anything, but it is a favorite excuse. Grow up!

We are not as easy to deal with as your Spiritual Guides, and we expect it is because teachers are onto the tricks of students. You may not like to be held back, but if it improves your soul, you cannot deride us for doing it. If your soul is to be returned to Earth, we will offer no explanation. The excuses are always of your own making, but Spiritual Guides often abet and aid their souls. If your life is not going well, you should seek them now. When your life goes extremely well, you believe you did it all. If your life falls off the face of your world, you believe God did it. Why? If one set of outcomes is yours, why not all?

There may be a few who are not listening now, but most of you do know that listening to wisdom is the easiest way to conform to the rules and pass the test. Life is always easier once you know the rules. Take time to develop rules that are easy to remember—then live by them.

Seek out those who believe as you do and advance. If your life is easy because you set out to do lesser tasks than another—that is the life you lead. If another person chastises you for not setting out to do more, you can safely ignore them. However, if you chastise another for living a more difficult life than you, we will not let you progress.

The telling of the tale is much easier
Than living the life that preceded it!

When your life is not as easy as it was, you often panic. If life grows easier, you believe it is because you planned it that way. Either concept is faulty. You do live the life you plan, but it may not be as easy as you planned. If your life grows easier, it is because you are being rewarded. No one else need be replaced by you. No one else need lose anything for you to gain. If life is rewarding you, all others have what they need while you are given more.

If you aspire to be rewarded, look to your inner growth. Live in the shadow of the tree and you will see the sun is not as warm there. If you aspire to greatness, you must sometimes live in the sun. The sun is hot and can burn, but the tallest of each species grow there.

It is not a sin for anyone to hide their abilities out of modesty, but to boast and brag as many do today is a sin. We would like you to believe in what you do, but not sell it. If other people want what you have, they will come to you to get it.

If produce you grow is not eaten, do not grow as much. If your life produces unacceptable goods, improve them until the public demands more. These are basic principles of superior societies. Why would a superior society reflect on following any other method of trade?

Now that the work of your life is determined, and it should be if you are closely following the work we delivered through *The Scribe*, we can begin to exceed the work of this plane and prepare you for the next one. That will be the goal of another book, but you can begin to anticipate it now.

Work on the following exercises and develop a rhythm that appeals to you. Once the work goes well, you can assist others. We will help you.

EXERCISES IN DEVELOPING SELF

1. Direct your eyes to the wall in front of you. Look deeply into the world there. Do you see beyond the wall? Can you see? Are you limiting yourself? Welcome the possibility that you can and will pass between the world and the wall. Look deeply into it again. Do you see any holes? Look in the middle. Does it reflect? Does it appear thin? Does it look any easier to penetrate? Walk over to the wall and touch it. Does it feel solid? Why? Can you materialize a wall now? Yes, you materialize walls constantly. You constantly create barriers, but can force yourself to stop. You continually hinder your progress. Why? Fear! You believe you could not be anything but what you are. This is a wrong belief. You are *you,* and only your beliefs while here make you seek elsewhere. You live in your mind. Live free of fetters and your life is free.

2. Put out a bulletin to everyone in daily contact with you. Tell them you are going to change. Tell them you have decided to improve your life. Tell them you are now happy. Announce the day you will begin this new life and how you will do it—then wait. How many people are thrilled about it? How many ache to tell you how to live your new life another way? How many desperately try to persuade you to stay as you are—even if you are unhappy? Count how many love you. **Remember:** No one who loves you wishes you to be miserable.

3. In the bulletin above, add a recent picture of yourself and show how much you want to change. Paste another picture and indicate it will be you soon. Do you hear laughter? Do you see anyone sneer? These are enemies. How easy it is to discover them!

4. Put your arms around the next person you meet. Does he or she withdraw from you immediately or seek shelter? What if this person crumbles, would you have otherwise realized they had a problem? Why not?

5. If your life is not easy, place it on the table in front of you and dissect it. What looks old, dark, or ugly? What looks luscious? Put the old, dark, and ugly stuff aside. Serve up the luscious concoction. We want you to enjoy life!

6. There is a place in the corner of your room where you can sit and relax. Make it a nest. Put on our favorite music and let it wash over you. Really enjoy sound. Really enjoy sitting still. When your legs begin to tingle, we will help you sit on the floor. The floor is the best place to view the entire room, because it is low and everything is above you. Once you learn how to look up and measure the room with your eyes, you will see it is larger than you previously thought. Life is the same. Make sure you lower yourself enough to remain conscious of the size of your life.

7. Pull at your hair—strand-by-strand. Does it feel like much? Does it hurt? Welcome the sensation of pricking your scalp, but do not pull out a hair. If the hair is long, why not cut it? If it is short, why not let it grow long? It is your decision. You take responsibility for the hair on your head. If you neglect yourself, it is apparent. If you pamper or spoil yourself, it is also apparent. Put your life together and match it to others around you and you will see your life conforms to theirs. We want you to decide for yourself. Ask no one whether your hair needs to be cut. Ask no one if you need a new style. Ask no one if your hair style becomes you. Be *you*! Can you do that now?

Each of these exercises is to be completed properly before you continue to the next chapter. If your life has not improved by then, we will take responsibility; but if it is improved, you may take all the credit.

Welcome change! Accept change in you and in others, too, as a way of growing beyond old ideas and stale ideals. If you do this every day of your life, you will be young at death, regardless of your age.

Chapter **Ten**

This is the time to begin new work—if you do not like what you are doing now. If your work pays well, reconsider making changes. If you are being treated unfairly or not paid enough, it is a sign you need to reevaluate your credentials. You must sit and review how your employer uses your time and if your time is well-paid by them.

Many people work for a lot of money, but few people are overpaid. Think of all you do. Do you live off your wages? Do you live off the wages of others, too? If your wages are not great enough to pay for all your needs, you are not earning enough and must seek another position. If your wants are met, as well as your needs, you have more than enough money. Having said that, let us look at the ways you can make more money:

1. Use your money to make money. Invest it and put it into the work world of another who can use it to create jobs for others if you cannot.
2. Enter another field. If your present work is not paying you to do it, it may be overcrowded now. Seek a less populated area or one where few people of your talents live. Develop into a larger-than-life figure and command more money. You can do all of this and not give up the work you presently do. It is best to start out from a secure base and add expertise as you move along, rather than walk out without thought and go into something entirely different.
3. Put your life in order. If your present life is not the problem, seek another avenue to express the real *you*. Put out feelers to

see if you are good in any particular field that could use all the abilities you are currently developing, before you think of changing fields or seeking another position.

4. Learn to live on the income you have. It is always easier to economize when you are employed then to wait until you are not. The art of management begins at home. If your life is a sieve into which much money is poured—and almost all of it goes down the drain, you cannot manage well. Admit it—then put your life on hold and write down everything you do. List your needs and what they cost *you* (spiritually) versus what they materially cost. List your wants. What are you willing to give up in order to fulfill your desires? Compare the two lists. Are you really poor or just downhearted?

5. If you lust after the rewards of this world, you will have nothing left for love. You must not lust after material goods. They are the fruits of labor—nothing more. If you crave them, make them. If you actually make what you want, you will want less and less.

6. Visualize your work sitting in a box—examine it closely. Is it piled high and threatening to overflow? Does it look good? Does it look like it should be thrown out? Place your life in another box. What does it look like? If your work and life are similar, you have harmony—regardless of the degree of disarray. If one aspect is in direct conflict with the other, you are in deep trouble. Prepare to evaluate such a conclusion. If it troubles you for several days, put an axe to the box and rebuild it immediately. Do not put anything into the box you do not want to keep. Life is short—but you live eternally. Live this life now!

Now that you know how to make money, you can begin to concentrate on why you do not like to work. It is not some deep, dark secret that people of your societies do not like to work. It is apparent! No one goes into the workplace and asks for more work. Instead, everyone asks for more money, or time-off, or benefits—not more work.

See yourself as others see you before you evaluate whether you are working as hard as you should work. If you work hard, it shows. You fear nothing. You know your work is good. You know you can sell your labor. You know you can turn out a product. You know you can honor the work of others and not be guilty of exploitation. But what do *you* do? Do you ask for more work? No, because you believe others do not work hard enough. You ask for more money because others are paid too much. You ask for nothing more than what you believe you are worth, but you think you are worth more than others.

Stop and look at the real *you*. Do you see anyone within who would stand up and shout at another? Do you see another person within you who wants attention? Do you see yourself selling *you?* What else could you see if you demand attention and pay for work you do not do?

Put your life in order before you shout about the salary or wages you receive. List everything! Lists are great for those who are orderly of mind, and lists help the confused, so itemize all you need and cross-off what you already have. If your needs are largely unmet, you need to work harder.

To put your life in order requires no money. It requires time and effort, yet some of you try to hire someone else to do it. How could you ever know *you* if you do not take time out to analyze your life? Psychiatrists are not doctors who prescribe medication for mentally disturbed people. They are arrangers of others' lives. They prescribe medication when the individual refuses to accept their life.

Realize you alone are in charge of your life. To place another in your place is to accept that this life is over. You cannot accept responsibility for anything else in life if your life is in chaos. You cannot accept challenge or direct your efforts toward anything of merit if you cannot do your work. Begin to seek help, but do not look to someone else—look within.

Now that this life is going well, how could you do it better the next time? Would you accept God at an earlier age? Would you meditate more? Would you concern yourself more with others? Would you ignore the passions of youth? What would you do? Now do them within your mind.

The only acceptable way to dwell on the past is to relive the past. To simply rehash and deny any responsibility for what you did is not helpful. You must remake the tape, reprint the photos, put your life in a better light, and stop forsaking God. It is easy to do!

Once you know how to use your past to its greatest effect, you can live now. To live now and accept the past as it was is the best possible way, but if you must remake it—fine. To grow you must live now. Your life stems from the past, but gains all its life now. So, if you accept yourself and live now, you will have a full future. If you continue to wallow in self-pity, denial, and refusal to accept responsibility for choices *you* made, you will continue to live in agony.

To deny your life is the safest way to stay confined to the one you live in now. Do not live, just sit. Do your thing. Do nothing for anyone else. Do not work on anything. Do only your work and never do anything extra. You can have that life. It suits you.

Whatever you do, do it with the verve of a person who has had a lifetime to develop and thrive. Once you appear to thrive, you will. It is easy to seek help if you do not appear to need it, but if you act down-and-out, and unable to put it all together, no one will offer help. Others recognize that which is within you which is like themselves. If they dislike the trait you expose to them, they will not help you. If you expect to lean on others, you must not develop negative traits. If you do, you will learn you are branded incompetent. No one will offer to help you, nor will you be able to blame them for it.

Whatever evil you did to someone in the past will have to be undone in the present, before you can accept the fact that it affected *you*. Your life is never upset by others. You do that to yourself. When you think about going to the store, do you think you will find what you are looking for there? If not, you have a very negative personality and little chance of finding what you want. You need to look at every aspect of your life to see who you really are.

When the sun goes down, do you wake up? You waste your life if you work all day at a job you despise, but it is your life. You can do what you like or not, because it is always your call. If you do what you hate in order to please your loved ones, they do not love you. If you do what you want and are despised, they are not friends. You should recognize that no one who loves you will ever want you to be unhappy, and if anyone wishes you well, they are a friend. All others are neutral.

Enemies of the worker are seldom obvious. The worker has many friends—few are enemies once they recognize the quality of work. To imagine your boss hates you is absurd. To imagine anyone would hire or continue to pay or want someone they hate is crazy. They would simply fire you and get another worker. You have to realize it is you who hates your boss.

If you hate a boss, you must analyze why. Does it come from the fact that he or she has a lot of money? Does it come from their misuse of power? Do you hate many above you? Do you envy? Are you seldom satisfied? If you say 'no' but know deep within that you are guilty of misjudgment, you will feel a knot in your stomach now. If your boss is guilty of misuse of power, this knot will disappear. How many knots do you feel now? When will you leave this situation? We will watch to see if you can take it.

Your first boss is the most important one, because you learn to hate or love the situation. If your first boss ignores you or despises your contribution, you will never love work. Fact: You are set up by your first job! Make sure you do your work at home to insure your first boss is on your side.

Put your life in order. Put your job in order. Put it all together. Now you are ready for a personal relationship.

Why wait to love? You need a personal relationship to enjoy life, but you have to make a life for yourself *before* you can enjoy being you. It is not difficult, but it does require maturity. To enjoy life and love, you must be able to substitute your life for another. However, to seek out another simply to avoid your present life is the worst possible reason to move into another person's life. It will cost *you* too much.

When your life is over, do you think you will remember people who worked with you? Probably not, because they too were working and seeking a good life then. But if you do think of them, who do you remember—those you hated or the dear ones?

Obviously, you want to be in good shape mentally at the end of this life, so you cannot dwell on those who disagreed with you or helped you end a life of total disabuse of others. You will remember you learned this or that from someone, and that another always helped you, and you were always happy to see another. You will remember those who helped you enjoy working and improved your work—not anyone who disabused you of the purpose of your work or caused you pain.

Whether or not you like work is not the purpose of this work. We are telling you of the relationships you must cater to now—not simply the ones you want for yourself. You cannot help but act foolish if you do not like those in power over you, so make sure you appreciate what they do for you.

It is not difficult to act with sincere goodwill when you are incapable of any other behavior. To ignore others who appear to be less prosperous than you is to be prideful and ignorant. You are not prosperous. You do not have more than another. You are not smarter, or wiser, or more desirable than all others.

You are a human who arrived on Earth to complete a mission. If that mission required a life of ease and intellect, you were given certain advantages to help you develop it. If your mission requires patience, understanding, and a lot of other intelligent choices, you will not be given anything, but will be allowed to accumulate. If you are here to learn from the past, you are definitely handicapped. It may be intellectual, physical, or emotional, but you can rise above it.

We want you to live this life so you do not have to return to relearn. If you refuse to obey the laws of God, there is no easy life. Your present life reflects *you*. Do you think it could do otherwise?

What we want from you is a life of tolerance and hard work. When could you harm or do evil to anyone if you lived such a life? We can count on you to successfully complete the lessons of this plane if you do these two things—that is why we pray for you to commit to the path of God.

When you seek out another for play, you seldom look at the way that person acts, but once the play is over, you know a lot about how they live their life. If you play fair and they do not, you will never trust them again. If you play unfair and they do the same, you will grudgingly befriend them. However, if you play unfair and they do not, you respect them. Respect is the cement and cohesiveness of any relationship—including loving ones.

Your life is a reflection of your relationships. If you follow the herd and never lead, you will become animalistic. If you develop your ability to be alone and lead if needed, you will always be wanted by others. If not needed or wanted, you do not have to stay where you are. The ability to move is essential to growth.

If you join a group of individuals, you will soon see *group-think* taking place. If the leader is egoistic, crude, or rude, the group acts the same. If the leader is enlightened and sincere, members become likewise or drop out. It is the nature of a group to adopt the same way of looking at things, so be sure you agree with or respect the leader when you enter the group, otherwise you may find you change into someone you do not wish to become.

What you need in life is a series of groups to control the growth period in which you are then progressing, in order to gain control over your life. You do not join Scouts or Guide troops as a toddler, but later. You do not join sororities or fraternities in grade school. If you are to grow strong, live each stage of development with your peers. Any extension of your abilities is recognized if it exceeds others within your peer group, but it will never measure up to a higher group or give you great satisfaction. To be completely satisfied you are doing well, you must see your achievement compared to others of similar background and experience.

Once your life is over and done, you will not be asked to answer for mistakes you made and corrected, but you will be asked to correct anything you failed to acknowledge or accept, because life is a series of mistakes—and because *you* know you, we want you to sit down now and analyze why you refuse to accept your actions.

When you complete the following exercises, you will have a clearer understanding of the need to be *you*, while letting others develop unimpeded.

EXERCISES BEING YOURSELF WITHIN A GROUP

1. Place your life within the work you do and see it as it is. Do not look at others' work or lives! Can you see *you*? Do you fear? Do you laugh? Do you want to continue working?
2. The previous exercise takes much time—and you need to do all of it before doing this one. Once done, put the life you led inside a big cloud and imagine that cloud floating overhead. Does it look like *you*? Do you see it as it is or otherwise? Do you fear it is a major storm brewing? What do you think will happen? Who will chase away the cloud? Let it disappear now.
3. To become a cloud is not as easy as it might seem. Practice doing it several times. You have to constantly merge with other clouds and then reemerge. Once the sky is covered in clouds, who knows you? Who cares? You are not the only one, but you still count. Let the light—not the dark of the sky become the background of your life.
4. Place *you* in the center of a cloud now. Do you sink into it and never reemerge, or do you remain seated on top of it? Put *you* in the largest group of clouds you can imagine and see if you remain on top. Did you disappear? We want you to be visible, regardless of how many clouds fill the sky.
5. To put your life on hold is to imagine you are not here, but elsewhere looking down at you. You can do this when you can place yourself on top of a cloud. Simply refuse to stop concentrating until you see yourself sitting on a cloud. The ego will grow tired of forcing you to do its bidding and will finally give way to your Higher Self, so you can easily visualize.
6. We will help you grow into a bigger version of *you* in order to see where you are now weak. Blow up a balloon. Sit and aim it toward the ceiling. Does it grow? Does it expand? Work on

seeing the balloon move. Do you fear it will burst? Such fear can keep you from being all you can be. Now let out the air. Can you see how much bigger the balloon is now—even when deflated? You grow every time you stretch your limit.

7. Put your life and work on hold. Now place your friends on a cloud. Put your life-time friends on one side and then add the rest. Why are there so few remaining from the past? Who from the past still refers to you as friend? Put them in front of everyone. Now add one new friend at a time. Do you see anyone as being bigger than the old one? You need to remain the same. Ask the new friend to meet the old one. Do they like one another? Why are you sure they will not be friends? Accept *you* now! Let the past merge with the present and know new friends will be coming along soon, but to remain true to your life's path, you must hold onto who you are.

Include all of these visualizations in your meditation work. Remember to do them whenever you fear you are being swallowed by others. If you continue to see yourself separate and apart—unable to merge with others, you will have trouble in this world. You must work on being acceptable to others. You are not accepting your work or life if you cannot accept another; but if you accept others over yourself, you are in major difficulty, because you refuse to believe you are of God.

Put yourself in the place of others, if you have difficulty remembering that they, too, have problems. You can become myopic and disbelieve in others. If this happens, you will not have friends. If you are to be remembered, you must develop into the best possible friend. If your life is a solitary pursuit of being you, you will never know if you changed. You need others to reflect who you are. Your friends, business associates, and others are the biggest source of miracles in your life. Let them share the sun around you.

Whatever you do, know you are doing well if everyone around you is also doing well. You cannot be a success if others within your society are doing badly. We will not belabor that point now, but it is the basis of any organized society. The bigger the world, the better the life of the lower classes—or there is no true society.

Chapter **Eleven**

Put your life on hold, then sit still and read this. Do not move your eyes from this page. Look at the words one-at-a-time. Do you feel yourself slowing down? If so, you are too tense now.

Put your fears on hold. Do not say you cannot do this. Put out your hand now. Does it tremble? If it does, you are afraid of this material. If it does not, you fear it not. Let us now go into why anyone would be afraid of reading material channeled by a higher source.

Your relationship to God is the primary one! If you do not have a real relationship with God, you have no life—only a physical reality. To absorb all the depth which is *you*, you need to develop emotionally, as well as spiritually. To develop spiritually is not easy.

When you live in a town where everyone is on the same wave length, you are noticed. If you live where all are going in different directions, as in a large city, you are not recognized. Since you do not know anyone, you are not expected to conform. You can be yourself, but are you?

'Work in the city and live in the country' became the creed of many generations. This belief became confused over time and altered the life patterns of many people. It caused much mental anguish and trouble within families. You cannot exclude the breadwinner. You must live near enough to work so the breadwinner can easily arrive home as often as necessary.

To seek a separate existence is to live alone, regardless of whether or not you are married and have children. You cannot grow up and out of your being without another to help you expand your belief system. You alter you, but do not know enough to enlarge your life. You need stimulation. You need new ideas and ideals. There is nothing within you that cannot be of use to another at some time. You have nothing within you that should not be shared. So why not share?

When you seek solitude, you may not know you are seeking *you*, but you are. Place your mind outside and let a rush of wind sweep away the cobwebs. Place your heart on the table and operate to remove all the dark spots. You are in charge of what lies within you. *You* will never be entered by another!

If you let others make up your mind about your religion, you are not in charge of you. You seek to have your life defined by another, which cannot be of worth to your divine Spirit or eternal soul. You need to seek your spiritual depth and appraise it. Do you value You (the Higher Self)? Do you think it is valuable to you? Are you aware of many others who are much like you? Could you shine in the proper setting? Do you need to be tumbled like a stone to knock off rough corners to look your best and shine? Are you smooth? Are you well-liked and selected before others? Welcome such appraising thoughts, but do not think too long on them.

When life is gone, and you know not who you are, you will be stunned to discover others also knew themselves well. You believe you know yourself as well as others, but you are wrong. There are millions who know exactly who they are. You cannot exclude yourself from the hoards of people now entering the new work.

Begin by putting your life on hold...

To place your life on hold does not mean you do no work. It means you stay where you are until you know where you should go next. If you rush from stop-to-stop—never looking at the station—you become lost. Instead, stop, keep your eyes open—and look at what is going on all around you without preventing your life to change.

Focus your eyes on the carrot and you will go no further than the driver allows. However, if you are the driver, you can determine speed, direction, and when to stop. You are unhappy if driven, so put your energy into the journey and let go of worry. Where you end up is the decision of the driver. If you let others steer, you will arrive at the end of their line, which may not be your goal.

You need to remember where you want to go! If steering, you should take into consideration the destinations of all who are along for the ride. If in charge, stop whenever someone must leave, and make sure they safely reach their destination. Do not run off and leave others stranded!

Your life was aided from time-to-time by those who helped you find your way. Do you do that? Seek out a way of life that is not strenuous. You need to flex your muscles, but not every day. Everyday work is hard if you are not prepared for it. Be sure you can handle your chores with relative ease, or give them to someone else.

Once you are in your niche, reach out to those still struggling and give them a hand. If you refuse to help others when asked, your perch will shake and fall. Within a career there are times when you cannot help others, but usually you can. Be sure you are safe before reaching down to pull up another.

Whatever you do, work out a map first. That map will help you design a life you want—not what someone else decides is good for you or for them. Parents often decide everything for their children, hoping they can spare them trouble, but in fact they hurt them. Do not try shortcuts until you understand why it is a shortcut. The long way round is the long way, but it teaches many required behaviors. You need to know why you do something before you can cut out excesses. If you do not, you will be bled dry.

To seek a source of pride through another is a common reason why parents abscond with the childhood of another. Never force a child to do what you wanted to do. You have another life. You can come back if it is that important to you. We do not advise it, but you can. If your children are forced to do what is not in their minds, you set a bad example. You are a tyrant. You are unloving and truly egotistical.

The egoist is one who does not care what others say about his or her actions. The egotist is not at all concerned about anything others feel. You have to begin early to weed out such evil from the mind of a child. If you do not, you doom that one to a life on another plane where lessons are less palpable than on Earth.

You worry about yourself!

You worry about those close to you, but never worry about those different from you, describes the egotistical egoist. There is no more concise and definite definition than that. Let us explain. You always need help to be you, but you have no need to help others. If you never help anyone else, you live as though you were royalty. Royalty pays the price of being looked up to all their lives. If they fail, the public will disgrace their names and humble their lives. You are not royalty. You live on Earth. You are no different than other humans, nor are you so despicable as to be less than others.

You need to recognize that your life is your life, and no one else is to be given your recognition or blamed for your failure to be the best you can be. You need to organize your thoughts and understand your relationships before you can see your parents are not responsible for you once you leave their protection, and you should leave their town of kindred spirits at some time in your life in order to know exactly who you are.

You know you are reasonable and honest—yet distrust others? Why would you dislike people you do not know? You cannot explain it, but you fear them. Your fear is what keeps you from developing further. Your fear is so intense it cannot be described, and you hope we do not analyze fear. It is that frightening to most of you! We will take it up in another volume, but fear is the enemy.

Once you love all you are, you fear no one!

Does that sound weird? You can sit and dream up a place where you are not afraid—but why? We can eliminate all fear in a moment, but why limit your growth by making it so easy? We want *you* to eliminate all fear. It is your life and your goal!

You cannot begin to understand who you are as long as you fear *you*. Some metaphysical teachings are weird. We admit it, and you can deride them, too, but you have to understand who you are before you can deride anything.

What do you think happens if you cannot accept the teachings of death as channeled for generations? Do you have another theory? Why not publish it? Will it stand up to generations of differing viewpoints attacking it?

When you finally understand who you are, you acknowledge God within all others. You do not attempt to attack them or deride them in any way. We want you to help and do a lot of work—but not against us. If you advise everyone you meet that your life is now so much better than it was because of a different diet or career, you are not helping anyone else, and your gifts of The Holy Spirit will be less and less noticeable then.

What you need to do when you find a way to lessen your burden is listen to what another says. If that person is asking for help, give them the benefit of your experience. That is one time when you would not be considered as being egotistical. You cannot force your beliefs onto others, but to refuse to help is also a sin.

When you hear evil of another and wish it would stop, do you repeat the message? If you do, you are not stopping it. You cannot repeat a message of ill will without becoming part of it. Much gossip is in the nature of information being informally transmitted, but some people use these avenues to transmit their own venomous thoughts. You need to be aware of the truthfulness of the one who starts the chain. If you question the merit of the message, it is probably unwise to repeat it. If the message could help another avoid serious problems and you do not repeat it, it will be your fault if they lose. You have to make the decision.

Once you pass on thoughts, doubts, misinformation or worse, you are held responsible for it. The world is now so full of false witnessing that all are guilty. What do you do if guilty of gossiping and harming another's reputation or means of making a livelihood? You have to make full reparation! You must pay for what you do.

No one knows you but You!

If you let a major disappointment destroy your sense of appreciation for all you have on Earth, you are prone to disappoint others. The disappointments of life are no excuse for disappointing those who believe in you. Your life is held up to the light at crossing over and you are held in contempt by *The Judges* if you cannot explain why you never apologized to people you hurt. You must do that! You must not let the sun set on your disapproval. If you hate, it grows into a massive structure within you and sometimes kills you. If your heart aches, you can offer it as sacrifice. Your body has many ways of wanting you to offer apology, but only you can do it.

Work for a living, but be sure it does not cost you your life. If you do work that shortens life, you will never know why you came to Earth. If your life on Earth is shortened by another, it is on that person's soul. If you ever consider suicide, you will be unable to return to Earth. You will be cast into the plane where immortality is not what you want. You are not to induce such suffering on your soul.

Working on life hereafter is not the reason you came to Earth. You came to do some specific task, plus the other three jobs everyone must complete before you can advance to the next plane. We will quickly run down the three primary reasons you came to Earth:

- To work hard every day of your life on living a good life.
- To socialize and learn to tolerate all other people.
- To do evil to no one—even when tempted.

Now that you have been reminded of the tasks you *must* complete, let us continue to the next work.

After all these tasks are done, you are given additional work to do. We refer to it as a 'call' or 'calling', but you may use other terms. Once you are *called*, you are unable to choose a different path. Accept it only if you wish, but once you do, it is not given to another. You are expected to complete it alone. If your life is not your life, you will never be *called!*

There are people who say they have been *called*, but are merely boasting. You will not boast, because it is not proper. You can boast only about trivial matters that require you to seek another to help you—a sort of recruitment tactic. Men or women who hold up their lives as an example (either good or bad) are boasting. You will not be persuaded that way, because your life is different. Please remember this!

When you listen to a man or woman boast, you reject half of what is said. You audit and cancel out what is egotistical or egoistic. We want your words to be accepted. We want your lives to be accepted as models of decorum and life as it should be lived.

If you let us help you live daily, you help us. We can easily do a lot of spiritual work and never interfere in your life, but you have to ask us to help you. We cannot intrude or enter you—ever!

If you believe spirits can enter the body of another, or even yourself, you are harboring a deadly fear held over from your ancient religious background and ingrown worship of that which is not of God. How will you ever advance if you believe God is evil and would harm you? It may sound strange, but why do you fear you are so important that God would want to tempt you?

We know of no human who has ever been tempted by God—not even Jesus. The stories of olden days have been diluted and changed, but not always for the better. You need to reevaluate your belief system—not let others scare you with theirs. If the time is not yet here for you to accept that God does not want to interfere in your growth, you will not grow.

If you are ready, we will continue. Work on the ways of Earth, then seek the ways of the upper realms, but do not seek work above when you have a lot to complete below. If you do, you are not taken seriously by those below or above.

If ready, you will be 'called'

You do not need to seek additional *psychic development*, since that is not the path of true enlightenment. It merely masks the ego. When a personality seeks *'enlightenment'*, using your Earthly terms, you cannot know where they will end. In our realm, we know.

We are aware of that which is below us—but not above. You are the same as we are—but beneath us. As a result, we see things differently, but most of us have been in your place. Do not fear something because you cannot see it, instead fear fear.

Since the relationship between man and God is under discussion, when do you seek God? Why? Where? How often? In what way? We refuse to limit you! We never enter into your worship. You can worship. You are required to worship. You will be held responsible for your worship. We are not requested to help you worship!

Place your life in the middle of your forehead as if it is a piece of white cloth. Hold the cloth with your left hand and place your right hand over your heart. If your heart beats louder than usual, you are strongly urged to remove the cloth. If your heart beats as always, continue with this exercise.

Put your mind into the cloth. Imagine you are outside your body living in a cloud. Place your life in the folds of the cloth and let it hang freely. Shed all your worries into the cloth. Place your life on top of the cloth, then put below it all other lives you feel are intertwined with yours. Why is the cloth getting dark? Are you upset? Do you feel you have too many people in your life? Why? What is it you fear? Are you feeling any relief? Do you see the cloth lighten—into white? Are you able to shed some of the people around you? Are you feeling great now? Let it continue brightening until you no longer fear what the cloth represents. Let it wipe out the past.

Visualization is the preferred tool of many seers, but few lay people use it today. We wonder why that is, but are aware many think it employs some outer power. How can that be? Does an outer power (whatever that means) employ you and your mind? Does an outer power use you to gain life? Are you stupid, thus an outer power passes tests for you? Who is this outer power? We want to know!

Now that your ignorance of power is exposed, when do you plan to educate your mind? We want you to teach, but you cannot teach if you know nothing. Seek out the best—the most knowledgeable around you—and learn. Ask them not why they believe, rather seek your own answers.

We will begin a series of classes and help you learn from them, but first let us end this chapter with two exercises.

EXERCISES TO GAIN YOUR BALANCE

1. Place your hand before you. Put it on your body anywhere. Where did you put it? Above or below your waist? In or out of its usual resting place? Away from you or close to you? When you hide, where do you seek refuge? Is it enclosed or open?

   Now visualize you are driving a big truck. Where are you headed? Are you alone? Are you carrying a full load, half-load, or no load? This determines the speed you will travel. You cannot travel fast with a full load. Now let out all the air in your tires. Can you push the truck? Not if it is over-loaded, so take out whatever prevents you from pushing the truck. Leave it by the roadside and walk away.

   Lastly, put your house up for sale. Advertise it as a great place to live. Tell all who look that it is not your home, but you know it is great. Live in the house. Sort through the closets (mentally or physically) until you find all you want—then place all useless things on the curbside.

   Now that you have visualized it all, put your mind to work removing all the old, useless, out-of-date material and beliefs of no further use to us or *you*. Place all of it on a seaport dock and watch it sail away in a ship.

   Life is so much more relaxed and accommodating to those who are not overburdened. Why sit, or lag behind others, because you think you are supposed to be overburdened—as if it is your karma or something? You are here to be *you*. Live now!

2. Sit still and let your mind rest. No need to visualize or philosophize now. Exhale the stale air in your lungs in exchange for clean fresh air. Repeat to remove all the stagnant air. Do not reenter that space until the air is clear. If the air around you is not clear, why are you sitting there?

Sit with your feet up on a stool. If you have no stool, use anything to elevate your feet. It is important that your feet not touch Earth. Now let your mind become still. Put your life on hold and breathe. Do not sing or shout—just breathe. Are you calmer? Do you feel better? Are you upset? Do you constantly fear disruption? It is all in your mind!

Now don your usual face. Are you smiling or unhappy in appearance? It takes tremendous energy to frown, because you have to suppress a smile. To be positive is the normal object of the mind. You are positive light beings who came to Earth to learn to accept and react to negativity, but it is not meant to overpower you. If overpowered, you do not accept anything. Feel positive energy emerge and take over your mind and body now.

Open your eyes, you are a new person
You can do it all!

Do whichever exercise turns your life around now. One exercise may not always be the best for you, so as years go by use both to restore your sense of equilibrium—which is absolutely essential for inner peace.

We will go forward to help you remain peaceful and serene. If you permit, we can still the waters and quiet the sea, but only you can choose to remain calm and cool. We will help as much as we can to clear the debris from your path, but it is *your* path! Know we exist and that you have no need of human help, but why deprive yourself of every helping hand you find?

Chapter Twelve

The correct way to begin working on anything is to start at the beginning. If you start half-way through a work and attempt to carry it out, you will be constantly reminded that you have not covered all the material. For this reason, we do constantly remind you that you must start at the beginning of our work here.

You cannot jump in at this point and expect to understand the totality of this work. It will require an act of faith and result in a jumbled conclusion. We want you to *know*—not just believe us!

To know yourself is the greatest achievement in this world, but seldom do you find anyone who accomplished it. We congratulate you if your life has shown you your weaknesses, strengths—and the difference between them. We will help those who struggle to determine why you are unable to achieve this life's promise.

First you achieve, then you analyze why you succeeded. Once you fully understand your conclusions, based on the knowledge of your strengths, proceed to analyze your weaknesses. Weakness is seen as the opposite of strength, but actually it is part of the same continuum. If your strength is that you are persistent, your weakness is that you are stubborn. Do you follow us? We want the truth to be known about you. If you analyze your abilities, can you remain honest with yourself? We doubt it, so we are offering you help now.

When you sit down and relax, do you meditate?

We see you hesitate—and now you doubt. You wonder, '*Why would I meditate now?*' This sort of reasoning happens each time you question yourself. For that reason, we want you to think of nothing now—act like a robot and blurt out the first thought or word that pops up—no thinking about the sense of it. Once you learn to blurt out what comes to your mind, you will find it easier to talk to everyone, because you will be telling your truth. It takes years to discover you ceased to tell the truth in an attempt to cover up weakness.

When you talk of truth, you usually include what sounds good or is inoffensive to listeners, but we want you to speak openly of what you feel. This is the only truth. When a person speaks from their feelings, everyone knows it. The crowd is electrified.

You may have to control the beating of your heart and soul as it responds to honesty. This is what we want you to do: Speak of your life in sounds that reflect *you*—not overwhelming others with blasts of hot air and sounds that deafen them. Your ears are not only instruments of hearing, they are also instruments with great ability to pierce sound and divide it into pieces of intelligence the mind can absorb. If your mind is dead, you hear no sounds. If your hearing is impaired, you have difficulty managing to understand others. It is vitally important that you never blast the ear until it can no longer hear. We will show you how to provide relief for the ear in a future volume.

Whenever your heart aches with the sorrow of life and you believe you cannot go any further, do not seek relief—seek help! If your fellow man cannot lend assistance, you always have Spiritual Guides. These Guides are not of Earth, but reside here. You are never far from them. We speak of their help and know they are with you even as you read this book, but you may be unaware of their presence. For this reason, we devoted this chapter to contacting Spiritual Guides who reside within us and live within our plane. Yes, we have Guides, too. No one in God's worlds has to travel alone.

To begin the first lesson in contacting your Guide, we suggest you relax more than you are now. We will help you establish contact, but first you must know how to relax and breathe easily. These two aspects of your life are often neglected. Since you exist in the flesh, you have to work harder with your Spiritual Guides than all other entities to be receptive to their intervention and assistance.

Put your heart into this work. Put your mind into this work. Put everything you have into the work of the world—then be able to retreat from it. Never retreat while sitting within the world, since it could leave you unprotected. Always sit in your safest haven before retreating from today. We suggest you seek a safe haven before you read and work with this material.

Bow your head as you read this!
I DON'T UNDERSTAND

Do you see how much your mind absorbs? You understood. You knew exactly what was written. You even knew that you understood. We want you to know that when you say, *"I don't understand"* that *you do understand.* Now let us begin again…

How do you learn to explore your mind? You begin with the first thought that comes through your mind. Seek out an idea. Learn its meaning. Sit and develop the ways in which you can drop that idea without leaving it. Will you learn more if you let it sit and come back to it later? Yes. If you seek answers, you need time to search the files within your mind and within this universe. It may take more effort to find the answer than you are ready to accept, but once it is found—you know it forever.

When the work of one mind is not enough, the minds of others will be used to construct your life. If your life is of worth—all lives originally are—you do not know how many others contributed to it, but within a few years you should be able to recognize it. We would appreciate if you all accepted that you, too, must make such contributions. If you stop and take only enough for yourself and never put anything back, how many years before the stockpile is depleted? This is occurring on Earth now.

You need only things you cannot exist without now. You do not need new clothes until old ones are no longer of strength and warmth. You do not need much food if your body is round. You do not need to work on the body if it is strong and your heart is good. However, you always need to develop your mind. Your mind has no ability to develop itself. It needs you to constantly fill the vacuum. Once your ideas are located and developed by you, others around you will influence you, but only God can change you.

When Earth begins to wobble and shake, your hearts are astounded. Why? You live on a living organism and it breathes, too. Would you be startled to be awakened by the noise of your father snoring? We would hope not. The noise of Earth is not to be feared, either. It is the noise of your kind that is fearful. We want all this noise you produce to be deadened or made beautiful. Why would you send such discordant sounds out into the universe? You are not well then. You cry to the heavens, but it is your noise that sickens you. We will never condone this as self-expression. You need to believe us now that you are not who you think you are. We say *believe* because you cannot know that until you are no longer in flesh.

When your hearts overflow with joy, you hear nothing. Why? We want you to sing when you are happy—not when you are sad. Sadness is not a longing for satisfaction—it is self-pity. Put your life into a song and let all know you love them. Once the love shines, your life is better.

We want you to do something unknown now. We want you to sit where you are and sing of a time when you were happy—sing out of tune or whatever, but sing. After you let out this little song, another song will erupt. You must not stop singing now. We want you to open your mouth and let out a sound. You cannot, because you are mute? Even the mute can sing! We know that. We can hear.

You need to sing. You all have voices that reach high notes and drop to low keys, but none of you sing enough. Once a person sings, all other noise is lessened. You can hear and breathe better. We want you to know this now so you can open up your life to your Guides.

Your Spiritual Guides are not deaf or dumb, but you could be. What you need to do is sit still once your Guides are alert to the fact that you want them. If your body has been very lively for years, you need to still it. Once the body is still and you are relaxed, your Guides will enter your thoughts. They will *not* take over your body! They will *not* enter your mind! They are energy and electrify *you*! If you ever saw a lantern that formerly used kerosene for power and is now electrified, you will recognize the difference between living without your Spiritual Guides and living with them.

If you put your Guides in touch with the Spiritual Guides of others important to you, you then need do very little personally to maintain a close rapport with them. However, if your Guides do not approve of a relationship, you cannot expect any help from them. The work of your Guide of this life is deep and personal, but there are also others who assist your Guide and dedicate a major degree of energy to you. If you doubt this, you have not yet made contact. Get busy on that!

When a Spiritual Guide of great development is assigned to *you*, you will notice your life becomes elevated from whatever it was. You will now speak in grander terms and react in a cool, calm manner. If you are required to do great work, you will have the assistance of the higher realms.

Why would you be afraid of the (personal) Guide who is here to assist you in attaining the next plane? We are not sure you are aware of this now, because many of you talk as though your Guide is on another planet. You live on Earth and your Guides are here with you. You may not see them or believe they are here, but they are. We can see them as easily as we see you.

When humans cannot see something—visually, they often become so irritated or confused that some of their mind is lost. Why do you question when a substance is not visible? Oxygen is not easily detected, but you do not claim it does not exist and that anyone who believes it exists is in danger of losing their immortal soul. You have to believe in your ability to know what exists and what does not—even if invisible.

The only time we know for sure you are upset is when you cry. We cannot understand why you get upset, because we do not get upset. If you care a lot about someone, you cry. If you hate someone, you cry. If you are angry, you cry. We ignore the tears if you cry a lot; but since most of you seldom cry now, we listen to see what may be wrong.

The work of the world is not the work of the next plane. It exists here and nowhere else. You could be doing this work on another plane, but you elected to come to this one. Your Spiritual Guides elected to help others and were then assigned to you. You do not select your Guides. Usually, you do not know your principal Guide, but may recognize other Guides from previous life episodes in which they were assigned to help you then and continue to pray for your salvation now.

The saving of one soul is the message of *The Church* in your world, but it does not mean the same thing to us, because you are not a single soul. You are many dimensions within a single entity, and your soul is the entire entity. If you have only one personality in this world, and that is true for many of you, you have only one life to live. But if you have several lives going on at the same time, you may not be able to clearly define which life you are working in now.

This dimensional split causes headaches and pains in the region of the spine due to the re-creation of each cell each time you jump from one personality to another. If your life is dull and listless, yet you are always exhausted as if working hard, you may be living a very fulfilling life on another plane. We can see some of you are aware of this, but others are puzzled by it. Your world has withheld so much information from its people that you no longer know the simple basics of life, so we will help wherever we see you are too lost, but we cannot fill in everything you want to know now.

If you want to talk to your Spiritual Guides, you need to meditate—and if you expect to hear their replies, you have to meditate. You can drive a car, dance, or do any activity while meditating, but for beginners it takes much concentration. We will now help you learn to concentrate and focus on this simple task.

To concentrate you have to deliver your full attention to one spot. If you cannot do this simple task, you have no business reading this book. You are a fraud if you say you cannot concentrate—yet are reading this book. Reading can only be done when you concentrate or focus your attention on the words. We will teach you to concentrate at a deeper level than reading, but it uses the same principle.

Begin by putting your hand over your eyes...
Do you see anything?
Do you hear anything?
Do you feel anything?

Obviously you still feel your hand—and your hearing is not diminished, so why say otherwise? We want you to concentrate on the sight you lose. Put your hands on the table or your lap and concentrate on keeping your eyes closed. Is it difficult to do? We hope not.

Now place your thoughts inside the mind. Do not let your attention wander about the world. Keep it inside your head. Pretend your eyes are open and you are staring into the space above and between your eyes. We are aware you refer to this as the *third eye*, but we call it your *point of reference* or *still point*.

Once you achieve this *point of reference* or *still point*, you can easily return to it anytime you prepare to meditate. With full attention on this point, you usually can see a human or animal eye. Do you see it now? Look until you see it. If you cannot see it, do not continue beyond this sentence.

Look carefully at the eye now. Did you decide if it would be human or animal? No, it is just an eye. Your eye looks like that of a cat, if you resemble a cat. Your eye is sharp or dim depending upon how well you see now. If your eye is clear, open, and large, you can begin to meditate on your relationship with spiritual beings who can steer you though this life and deliver you safely to the other side.

With a lot of insight and a little patience, you may be able to talk to your Guides without interruption at any time or any place, but for now you need to further develop your spiritual *'muscle'*. We will help you flex and stretch until it is strong.

Put your mind into the center of the area within your *middle eye* and let it dissolve. Do you see anything different having placed your life there? Do you feel anything different? Do you hear anything? Some will hear voices or what sounds like voices, others will see symbols or colors—but remember, whatever you get was not there when you began this work.

Once your mind is clear of the day's debris, you can more easily concentrate on your life. If the debris of your day is so large it cannot be ignored, we will help you chase all your cares away. Do the following with us now:

Imagine you are floating on a raft in the middle of a stream. It is a beautiful day and you are feeling lazy and unable to swim, so you let the raft drift. As it drifts, you dangle your fingers in the water and let the water wash over and through them.

As a thought emerges, let it follow the flow and leave you. Let each thought emerge and disappear. After a while, thoughts slow and finally disappear. Sit in stillness.

You will feel, hear, or see something that is the Holy Spirit moving within you. Let it speak to you of the route you should take now. Let it guide you to the source of your river of thought, and let the water be clear. Once you can easily do this, try to shorten the time needed to do it.

We want everyone to meditate, but some have so much static from being positive beings in a negative world that they cannot easily free themselves from it. If so, we recommend they enter into a commune until such time as they are free of the double dosage of negativity and can stand on their own.

For those of you who have great difficulty channeling your Spiritual Guide, you may have better luck seeking out another who is gifted in the area of channeling other people's Guides. However, that seldom results in permanent solutions, because so many channels would seek to make you dependent upon them—and we oppose that. If you have access to a spiritual channel, you may do so for a short time without harming your spiritual development.

Whatever you do, do your own work! Do not expect a spiritual channel to do your hard work. Use others to explore new areas or develop a higher order of guidance, but do your own work!

If you seek out others to help you, you can harm your development. You harm the development of others if you do their work for them. Therefore, make plans to learn to channel your own Spiritual Guides today—and then do it!

EXERCISES FOR CONTACTING YOUR SPIRITUAL GUIDES

If you skipped ahead to this section—ignoring all the work that precedes it—go back to the beginning of the book and start over. You will get no further ahead—may lose a lot of energy—if you do not begin at the beginning and work up to this point. For those ready and able, let us begin.

1. Place a plate of water on a table. Sit still and stare into the water. Do you see anything? Keep looking. Do you understand why you can look at water and not see anything? Are you sure you know who you are? Who is staring into the water? Do you see your reflection? Make it possible to see *you* now. Look at your reflection and ask it if you are now *you*. Do you see any change in the water—in your reflection? Do you hear anyone speaking to you? What do you expect to happen? Let the plate of water remain as is while you let your thoughts float away. Do you feel calmer now? Do you feel serene? If so, you have channeled your inner self.

2. Place a chair in a room where no one will bother you. Visualize a circle of white light around the chair. Put yourself in the center of the circle and sit still. Do your personal meditation, then begin calling for your Spiritual Guides. Do you see anything moving? Do you hear anyone? Look carefully at the corner of your left eye. Do you notice movement? If you do, your Guides are present.

3. Plan a day in which you are home alone—and remain indoors. Tell everyone you are away, but stay home. This is the best way to make your first contact without disturbance. If you are disturbed, you have to start over again. To begin, ease off anything tight or binding. Let your breath be easy and not strained. If your breathing is stained, clear your airways.

    To seek your Spiritual Guides, do the above exercises and then the following:

    Stand tall and hold your arms over your head. Do you feel a stretching sensation in your arms? Please do not lower your arms. Place your feet apart and let your head rest back or forward. You can now stretch to your fullest height. This is in preparation for your soul stretching as far as it can reach at this time.

    During your day at home, sit still as you invite your Spiritual Guides to seek you. You will find they are not available all at once, but will be once you set up a regular time when you can meet with them. Ask them to work with you to create a life plan you can use to develop to your fullest capacity. They will help. When words form in your mind, write them down. Do not edit this work until later—if ever. Write whatever comes to you then. Let it stand exactly as it came to you. At this time you may believe it means one thing and later realize it means something else.

4. If you can write out messages after a session with your Spiritual Guides, you can also write their words in a journal. Collect all your messages in one place and verify the facts and predictions as they happen. Was the information verifiable? Was it meant to be literal or imagery? Do you know why you were told whatever? Do you fear anything now? Welcome the

relief of knowing your life is not a chaotic event without real purpose or reason for being.

5. When your Spiritual Guides become a daily or weekly part of your life, you must not let them rule your everyday affairs. You are in charge of this life always! You are the personality who determines the path, the way, and the means of reaching your fullest potential. Your Guides are here to lead you or direct you to the easiest path for your goal to be achieved. You will not receive assistance if your goal is in direct conflict with God's will. God's will is that all people on Earth share in what has been give unto them. You work for it. You are required to cooperate, and you must not harm anyone getting to your goal.

6. The only way to achieve success is to first achieve peace of mind. If your Guides are active and working beside you, you will have peace and understanding. You do not have to ask for it.

Work out these exercises in the order given. Do not skip about these lessons—ever! If a teacher has prepared a lesson plan, it is to be followed. You are a student—not a teacher, and you have given no thought as to how knowledge should be presented, so let those who have, have their way with you today.

When you sit alone—meditate. Use your idle time for *you*. Let it grow and develop into a sacred time when you can ask for guidance, seek peace, or welcome the Light of God, but always use it wisely and well. Once your life is lived in the Light of God, you never fall!

Chapter **Thirteen**

It is time to weigh the evidence and check how well you are doing so far. Place your life's work on an imaginary scale and add what you think is lacking in order to make it more balanced or weighty. In other words, find out who you are now! If the weight of the world is greater than *you*, you do not devote enough time to working for YOU. We seldom see anyone who devotes too much time to soul work. If it ever happens we will let you know.

You never *have to believe*, but to say you believe and you do not is a lie. You cannot deny you believe in something, because you are then saying you accept that which you said you do not believe. It may sound confusing, but reread it.

What the world does to you is nothing compared to what you do to *you!* We see everyone on Earth compare themselves to one another. It is as if you see yourself in a race rather than of a race. Get this right— you are all alike! You all have the same kind of bodies. You all think alike. You all breathe air and sit to study. Why would you think another person had something you would want? Why would you think you had something different from others?

You must recognize the difference between each individual as individual, but not as a person of Earth. Everyone on Earth is here for the same reason, and you have to determine what it is. Some people honor their own color and not others, and we cannot understand this. It is very absurd to say someone is different because the shade of skin is unlike another's. It would place you in a position of being so attuned to outward appearance that you could not enter the heart of another to see the real person. To enter the heart of another person is difficult if you know not what is in your own heart, but once you know *you*, there are few difficulties.

We seek those who know. We want only those who can relate to others to help us. We are not here to recruit you or your friends and family. We want only a few.

Whatever is in the ether, there are still those who live only on oxygen. They will be the only ones who will have to leave Earth. You are shocked that there are humans who can live on other than oxygen? We wonder that you have not realized that already. It is apparent that many people who require pure oxygen are dying now. They cannot be here. You all put drugs and gases into the air in order to spread your particular brand of egoism, and it is killing many of you now.

Put the test to the test. Place your hand in a clean glass bowl of clear water. Let it rest there for a few minutes. Do you feel the water after a while? We suspect it goes unnoticed. If you cannot feel your hand in a bowl of water, how do you expect to feel air in your lungs?

We want you to express the desire to do things others cannot do. Once you grow and do many of the things you wish to do, we ask you to do our work, too. Do you want to do anything for someone else? Today not many do, but soon more and more will know it immediately frees them from selfish intent.

Place your mind at rest now. Stare at the floor. Do you see anything strange on the floor? Does the floor look strange? Are you able to sit and not be bothered by the floor? Why would you be bothered by air not of good quality? You are unobservant of it.

We will now let you decide for yourself if you live solely on oxygen or a mixture of gases.

Pace the floor until you can hear your heart beating. Does it sound like you are racing about? Do you feel any strength leaving you? Do you tire easily after a few minutes of fast walking? Are you now unable to concentrate? What are you feeling now—the best of health or the worst? You cannot enjoy life if you cannot breathe, so take time to increase the volume of oxygen in your room and in solitude breathe deeply outdoors. However, do not breathe deeply in congested areas.

Do you wonder why we are not upset about the wind, or rain, or erupting volcanoes? We are. We see they upset you, but the wind frees you of debris, the rain washes away negativity, and volcanoes erupt to free Earth of its pressures. How are any of these events of no use to you?

You never have a lot of time. Too often you say, *"I'm swamped. I have no time for myself. I don't know where the time went."* Why would you not know all about time? You invented it in *your* world, while previous worlds invented calendars. All of you are so into time, yet lack total knowledge of what it is. Why?

It will be better for all when the world decides to let time dissolve. Until then, we must work with you on the theory of time. You never could decide why you have a lot of time at times and not enough at other times. We know.

We are here to discuss your life and its relationship to time. Set your heart to run at an even pace and you are never disturbed; set a clock and place it on the wall and you are often disturbed. What is the difference? One is created by God and the other by man.

Would you want to spend your entire life on Earth tuned into time? We would think you would feel it to be a prison, but most adjust to it, and crave to know exactly what time it is. We dislike thinking the time of day is so important that you must begin life, go to bed, be awakened, or never stay up later than a certain hour, but most of you are addicted to time. To become less addicted, you must begin to see the world as a place where you are in charge.

You are responsible for all decisions made here. We are not here to change a thing. We will never be allowed to change you, either. We are here to question and behave as visitors to a strange land—trying to absorb its culture. You are natives of this strange land and unable to speak in any real way about the work your world must do in order to survive. We will translate your babblings and take them back to the motherland and explore your life in depth there, but you will continue as you are here.

Whatever the day, week, or month, you have a name for it. We think you must go a bit insane if a day or month is lost—and it often is. We cannot account for all our time, and we are not asked to do so, but you people do. Why?

When your life is finished on Earth, do you think someone calls up and says, *"It's time to go!"*? We believe you think that and would continue to do so, if we did not stop that belief now.

What you do on Earth is not accounted for on a clock. It is requested that you monitor your life and keep it on schedule, but the schedule is according to season—not days. If you feel young, your life is in its spring. You may have very few years and feel old.

This is the way to age: *Put your ideas into motion in your youth and let them lay fallow until you finish your life's work, then reap the rewards of your youth.*

Eat less and less as you age, because you need less. When young, eat of the work of the hand more than the land. As you age, eat more of the land and less of the hand. It is not difficult to discover what we mean—use your reasoning ability.

If life is over when you are young, why stay? If your life has a purpose that requires many years to fulfill, you will be given more than enough time to do it. But if your age and life are quite different, you will be unable to finish your job here and will have to return to Earth again. We want you to align your life with your age, so you can get all your work done on a timely basis.

Time is relative to each and every human. The clock does not register the same time for each of you. You cannot design a clock that tells the same time for all. It will tell one person to sleep and another to awaken. You will be unable to tell one person to use time one way and another to do the same. Neither person has a sense of the other's life, so nothing can be the same.

You must not know your time of death, because it would be of little use to you and might upset others who share your life. You would cause them to believe it was their time to die, too. No one ever knows!

Once the ordinary life is finished, death is merely a ceremony. But the death of an extraordinary human can be quite dramatic. We are aware you question the death of Buddha, Christ, Mohammed, and other saints of your world. Their deaths were extraordinary, but so are many others not as well reported. You will be unaware of the death of most people, but some will pass into the ether with less of a response than others. We will not bother to explain this now since it negates our purpose of discussing your life and its relationship with time.

What you *actually* do is spend your life on the job. You are never without chores. You do them or are required to return. We see most of you believe you work very hard, but few actually do. Why? Why would you think you work hard when you constantly sit idle? The only people who know they are busy are working constantly, but they may also be avoiding their work. Look at what you accomplish and judge for yourself. Does it match your effort?

As time creeps by on your calendars, you figure out the seasons. We imagine it would be obvious, but you choose to watch the calendar. Why would you plant flowers before the ground is ready? Because you saw the date to plant on a calendar and followed suit. What a foolish way to live. You need to watch the signs for planting, weeding, watering, and reaping—then proceed.

What you need and what you have may not be the same. Place your mind in control of your needs and align them now. You need only sort through your stuff and decide if you may want any of it in the future. If you have not used it by the time your next inventory arrives, you do not need more. Someone else can use what you have no need for—and you will be blessed for sharing your excess with others in need.

Your closets are the repository of all the material things you collect. Once closets are sparse and cleaned of all excess, you feel much better. If your life resembles a closet, you will feel better after sorting through and removing old, unwanted, and disused material. Place your mind in that mode and begin sorting through all your old ideas now.

Start with the idea of time...

When your life grows out of its roots, you need to prune the top back so it will not die. You cannot completely develop until your root system matches the top growth or obvious parts of your outer life. You have only enough time to do your work and then be gone. If you completely uproot yourself, you need time to re-grow roots. This takes time—and time is of the essence.

If your life is self-centered, devoted only to your work, you will never fully enjoy it. We know you think others would harm you or take your things, but we know it is you who steal from *you*. You do not change. You stay the same as in your youth. You try to water down your principles, but they stay the same as the 18-year-old you were when you graduated from secondary school. No one cares about the other person in your world now, but it can all be changed. It is your idea—not ours or God's—or anyone else's belief.

Put your life on hold for a second. Does a second mean a very short time, a split minute, or just a moment? Can we hear your heart? Do you? We know how long it takes to spend time in your dimension and be back in ours, but you do not know how long it takes to get your family out of the house. Why would you not know such a simple thing? You do not observe yourself enough.

Putting a clock on every wall is no way to learn to tell time. You just know. If you continually look at a clock, you will forget. We know you do not care for time to pass too slowly—it does not. It passes at the same rate, but you catch it on different wave lengths. Once you know where your heart is, you know where to watch in order to see it beat. But once you know time, do you know where to watch to see it pass?

Working on *you* takes time, but working in the world is merely a pastime. It is what you do to pass your time from birth to death of this body. Once you cross over to the other side at *death*, you fear nothing and remember not a thing about this time. You fear no clock, death, or any other measurement then. Why not start preparing now to avoid being controlled by time? It could save you much effort at the end.

When your body is tired, rest. If your body is not tired, look at the time you waste stopping because the clock says it is break-time. We would think intelligent beings would have questioned that concept long before this, but it does not occur to most of you to question anything!

What you need to do to avoid clock watching is to sit with your mind on your internal clock and demand that life not be too long for your body to live through. Once sure your body will last as long as you are to be on Earth, you will have few concerns about your body. Really!

We would grow antlers if we needed them, so would you. If you needed larger breasts or bigger penises you would have them. It is the custom now to waste time working on your bodies to make them look good to you, but we dislike such a waste of time and think the outcome is dubious. Why not spend that time and effort meditating? You would look better than before and with a lot less effort—and no money spent. Your body would please you then, and you would be less critical of everyone else.

In the inner recesses of each mind is a little clock that registers time. If you look at it, you will see it does not register time on Earth as you do. It looks like a meter. It has a few dials or features, but it does not click or chime the hour. You have to look at it carefully to determine if you are late or early. You have to sit still to hear it and know it is your time and not someone else's. Think only of YOU, and time becomes known.

Weather is not the same as time. Weather was created by God. Time was not. You can never accurately predict the weather. When you try, you are playing at being God. Let the weather come and go as it will. Enjoy the sun, ignore the sleet, prepare for the rains, and let snow pile up. You cannot fight the elements. Instead, put your heart into knowing who *you* are. All these simple little things like time and weather are known then. You cannot expect the mind to wrestle over and over and over again with things it learned many times ago.

We would like you to exercise caution when you develop your *third eye* or look deeply within yourself. You do not have any sense of time, but it frightens you if you are out of your body for too long a period. If it is a split second (your time), you fear nothing and do not recognize you left; but if your time away is long, you grow very frightened and believe you died. We want you to know you are not dieing if you leave your body, review your records, and decide you want to come back and relive some of the things you neglected to do, so you can go forward at the end of this life.

Near-death experiences are time travel. You are not dead. Only God can take your life! You will not go before that time. You may decide to enter a life of tortuous agony by taking your human life, but it is not your life to take—so you are not dead. You will not know if your life on Earth is over until it is. Many remain locked in the belief system that they are still alive—after they *die*, so it is considered a blessing if you let that lost soul know it is no longer alive. To let a lost soul know it is no longer alive requires no degree of bravery. It merely requires common sense.

If you feel an unseen, unknown presence near you, try to find out if it is a deceased entity trapped in this dimension. Ask aloud: *"Are you alive?"* No big effort to ask such a simple question. If you *feel* something, you will know. You must *feel* something. If you do, just say, *"You are no longer living on Earth. You must go to your friends who are waiting for you on the other side. They are all gone and waiting for you."* Repeat this as many times as it takes to free that entity. No big deal to do this and no reason to fear.

Whether or not you believe in *ghosts*, some people are not ready to die when their lives on Earth are ended. This is the result of a faulty comprehension of time. They think they will have a long life, but it ends much sooner than they planned. You need not mourn this event, since that person required little time to do his or her job on Earth and originally asked for a short time period in which to do it. It is you who are required to stay on Earth longer—not them. Once you know it is time to go, it is.

Welcome the unknown!

Do not try to succeed in frightening yourself. If you believe, it will become. If you imagine there are frightful demons and devils, there will be such beings in your mind. You are in charge of the contents of your mind, and if you fill it with garbage, you will retrieve only garbage from it.

When you play on your computers, you talk to it. You talk to it as if a person. You enter data, record events, and exit when done. You are unafraid of it creating anything other than what you entered and arranged to calculate or print. Why would you see a computer as a far easier concept to accept than understanding how your mind creates stories and works of art?

Whether or not you want this life is your decision. Many of you decide to neglect your lives in favor of living off others. You will then not be advanced! You may even harm such people. You cannot expect another person to live for you. You are expected to live each day of your life as if it were the last day. Once you can do that, you fear death no more!

The only way to understand your life is to understand time as you developed it. Once you understand why you do what you do, you can begin to change it. We will help you start to unravel your misconceptions about time now.

Follow each of these exercises with a short period of meditation. If you can meditate before starting them, it is more beneficial.

EXERCISES IN TIME

1. Put your watch on the shelf for at least one day—then forget it. If you cannot trust your mind enough to do your work and not be late for anything important, you are not in charge of you yet.

2. Pull out a calendar and mark today's date, then mark this date one year from now. Place a list of objectives you wish to achieve during the next year on the second date. Does it sound impossible to accomplish? Good. Do nothing more with that list. Leave it. Next year—on that date, review the list and see how much was accomplished without any further thought from you. This is the biggest test of your ability to see into the future of *you*.

3. Put your hands over your face and count to ten. Did the clock in your mind appear? See if you can count to ten and see it. Once you can visualize this internal clock, set your morning wake-up time, your breakfast, lunch, and dinner times, as well as your bedtime. You will then be all set.

4. Visualize pulling time from a bottle of sand—dropping grain-by-grain. Do you think it drops faster at one time in life than another? Obviously not, but some believe they live faster at times. You are growing when you sense time moving rapidly. If you ever see time move slowly—as if in *'slow motion'*—you are near death. You cannot deflect time or slow it down. Remember, you have a lot of time—use it!

5. Use your imagination and decide why you need to look at a clock. Can you think of many reasons? Can you laugh at some of them? If you do, you are ready to change.

6. Change your idea of time and you change! Your life is a series of events. From time-to-time, one event excludes all others, but usually events overlap and you know not when one ends and the next begins, and the next... Put a timetable together to coexist with the remainder of the big events in your life, (marriages, divorces, feuds, jobs, retirement, deaths of others, etc.). Do you gain a sense of freedom by doing it? You should. You will no longer fear such events. You can let each one happen and dissolve into the next.

7. Work on the event you currently are locked into—do it well! Do not try to escape until it is thoroughly over and done to *your* satisfaction. Once this event is over, sit down and analyze why you went into it so deeply to begin with and whether or not you would do it again. If you do this with everything you set out to do, you will enjoy your life.

Whether or not you enjoy your stay on Earth has very little to do with time, but not having enough time is the prominent excuse used today by most of you who do not enjoy your lives. Get your priorities straight—then enjoy life!

We will continue to develop the relationship between you and your world, but for now—please continue to dwell on time.

Chapter **Fourteen**

The only way you know if you can get along in the world is to live there. If you live in the outreaches of the countryside, you have no way of knowing who you are. This is the only time you will have on Earth, so live in the city. If the city is dangerous, clean it up! We know many now run away from other people, but this is why you came to Earth—to socialize and learn to get along with others. If you avoid all such contact, you come back.

If you admit that many imagine most of their trials and tribulations, and your life is so easy you have few unsolved problems, you are best-suited to form the forefront of the attack on urban warfare. If you cannot rule your town, live in one being abused and abandoned by the rest of society now. Clear out the debris and clean it up! To let acres of land in the center of any town sit idle is a waste of resources, yet greed protests: *It's cheaper to develop idle land.* Why? The city has its infrastructure in place. The countryside is needed for animals and crops. Why does man neglect all other beings? Greed!

If you left your house now and walked half a mile, how many people would you see? How many would you say a word to about the weather? How many would you ask if they had a nice day? How many are close friends? If you said very few, you are not alone. Most of you do not know anyone who lives nearby. Work on that.

We want you to understand that living among people is not the same thing as socializing with them. To ignore the fact that you are *you* and have a soul is the worst offense. You need to develop every aspect of your soul. You are here only once. It may now seem like a long time, but if you are wise, you are here only once. Once is enough if you work hard, learn to live with fellow humans, and do not seriously harm anyone enough to merit a return to Earth.

Working in your home is not work. The work of keeping you busy is your detail. You cannot expect others to come into your home and inspect it to see if you are working or not. Your work is seen only by those who enter it; and if no one is ever invited into your home, you work for you alone. To describe this as work is to imitate others and state you are as busy as everyone else when doing half as much as all who also work and keep their homes clean.

If you live at home and work there, you have two jobs—just as though you worked outside the house, but it is more difficult to keep the two separate. We would not like to work as some of you work, but if you cannot work outside your home, make sure it is inviolate where you work.

To call and deny you are angry is a mockery of the emotions you hold within and cannot accept. This inability to communicate to another how you feel is at the root of evil today. Most people are not interested in anyone but themselves. You need to drop this attitude and get into family-unit thinking again. To be alone and on your own does not promote happiness. Admit it and be done with the conflict.

We know of many who protest that their families have done much evil to them, yet they do the same thing to their families. How evil was it if you continue to do the same thing? We cannot believe you then.

Were you to find a difficult person in your home, would you think they had no right to be there? Why? You are not always pleasant, smiling, and happy—and seldom interested in the lives of others—willing to share your work's resources with them. Why should others not act the same toward you?

You believe you are different—
So does everyone else!

If your life is not as unique as you believe it should be, do not ignore the lives of others. You need to develop characteristics that set you apart from all others. Today that would be work of the highest order since so many are wallowing in gutters. Whatever you do, you will be seen as you—regardless of whether or not it is good or bad. You have your own identity. It is not the same as anyone else. You are known for being whoever you are. Why change to gain more attention?

People who do not like being ignored seldom pay attention to others. The only way to be forever universally accepted is to do something worthwhile. If your life is seldom worthy of interest by others, you cannot be admired. If your life is on the fringe—closed to others' view, you cannot be recommended for honors. Live in the open and dwell openly if you wish to be on top of the list of those who live in your area. If you are unable to top the list, do not sit and pull down those who are. It is obviously jealousy that motivates people to pull down those above them.

Today you demand respect. Why? Respect cannot be commanded or demanded. It is earned. Since so few work at a respectable job, you all fear you cannot be respected. That could well be why you are here. You must make up your mind whether or not you wish to have a lot of money *or* earn the respect of your fellow humans. However, it is not much of a choice to make!

When the work of your day ends, do you sit alone? Do you eat alone? Do you sit and eat while watching television? Why do that? If you have no friends, go out into the world. If there is no one at home, eat in public. Do not sit alone at home if you have friends and neighbors who are eating alone. The best way to make friends is to share—and food is the easiest way to begin.

We often see nothing accomplished. We look and look and see you doing nothing! Why? Are you so fatigued from your little earthly chores that you cannot be *you?* Would you think yourself lazy if you saw a picture of you sitting on a chair or laying on a couch doing nothing? Why would you guess others are busy, if you are not? You do not. You believe everyone is as idle as you are. It is infectious and destroys your life. Work at things that need repaired rather than drain your precious resources to pay another to do your home work. Sit idle never.

Go to bed if you are tired!

The day is coming when you will need to sit. The time is coming when the last day is upon you, when there is very little time left to correct the errors of Earth, but right now there is still air enough to breathe and water to drink. Enter the life of your planet by helping to extend the air and water for those who must return again

'Welcome to the new world' is the way you need to think now. You never remember the old one. This one is all you have. Reach into your life and remember why you came to do all you did. If you have been idle, you cannot remember much, but you can begin your work now.

Imagine putting all your work in a pile and comparing it to others. Can you see it? How many piles of work do you have—compared to others? If you know you definitely worked harder than all others, you may now donate your time to the world. If you still have much work to do, give up and donate your money—not your time, until you know your worldly work is done. You need not donate time or money—it is your contribution that counts, because you never know when you may need help from the society within which you live now. Remember, if your society is poor, it cannot help.

If your society is now struggling to cope with the hunger and unemployment of others, you need to reflect on how best to feed and employ them at the same time. Only a genius could decide where and what they should do now?? Farm! What about all who work on farms now? Work is never finished on a farm. Today farmers have to work elsewhere to pay for equipment and help. If you supplied both, farmers could stay home and supervise the work of those who are temporarily out of a job. We see no problem—do you?

Would you believe we have nothing to do? Obviously, we work! Would you listen to any entity who has nothing to do all day, yet approaches you to teach you how to live your life? Some of you do.

Live and learn is the proper way to advance in this life. To live and not learn is impossible. Work is not the same as living, but it makes it possible. You need to work on your concept of life. Many do not care about anything but the prestige associated with a job. Why? No one outside the work knows you. Without work you have no prestige.

Would you think it crazy or irrelevant to be chosen to be president of your country? You would, if you had no idea where you lived, yet some believe you can be a successful politician anyway. You see it as an easy way to control the lives of others and earn or steal a lot of money.

We always worry most over those who have power to change the world and do not. If you are most powerful, you are held in great contempt if you do not do what you are elected or appointed to do. God alone will have mercy on you if you do not do your job then.

Worry and work are not the same, yet what most do. You need to work. You do not need to worry about work. Worry is not conducive to activity. It defrays your energy and causes stress. You need to be concerned about having enough to eat and being able to pay anyone who loaned you money in one form or another, but you do not need to worry. Worry is a negative emotional response to the positive need to keep busy. You need to be yourself, and if you work, worry disappears.

Putting out a lot of work in one day and then taking off six days to recover is not working hard every day. You need to develop a rhythm and work habits conducive to having enough to do every day. People who purposefully delay work in order to have a day off are the same. They, too, need to work daily. We know many seek jobs where they can be let go seasonally.

Why would you want to be idle? You do not like yourself when you are. Your families are hungry and worried when you are. You act like a beast and behave as a lonely human when you are. Get a job or create one that keeps you busy all year long. Anyone who works hard every day and has nothing to show for it is either lying to the public or not spending his earnings wisely. No one can work every day and not prosper.

To begin a life without anything is no crime, but to end one in total destitution is. If you do not work, you have no one to blame for your poverty. If you are working and those not working destroy what you have, you still have knowledge you can pass from this plane with while they will return and return to work over and over for all they wasted this life.

No one is permitted to loot. No one is permitted to take another's cherished possessions. No one is allowed—even on Earth, to deny the right of another to his own work. In our realm, you will see it is the work of the world that decides the degree of the man or woman—not the wealth achieved.

When you decide to do something, you have a choice. You can do it well or not. If you decide to do something, why not do your best? We often see you do not know how to work or do anything right, but that is your choice.

If you do not know how to work, learn how to do it first. You have to work even to learn. Sitting at a desk and idling is as big a fault as later in life loafing on the job. Grades from school days tell the world you worked or you did not. No one with high grades is considered to be a loafer or idler; but if you worked hard and your grades are not high, you have to prove yourself to you. Working hard is not the prerequisite of life, but a purpose. If you do not fulfill that purpose, you return and return until you get it right. Why would you want to work, and work, and work to avoid working now?

In the years ahead many of you will learn to your sorrow that you had a lot of work to do and ignored or did not want it now. Your work is your life! If you do not do your work, you will feel sorrow. We know of no one who has worked hard all of his or her life who regretted retirement. Only people who worked little or ignored their families all their lives in order to be away at work are upset if they must terminate their careers.

Remember your families are your work, too!

If you wonder why we stress work in a book about relationships, it is because you do not live alone. You live everywhere. You live at work and at home, but your work denies you many opportunities to be *you*. If your life at work is terrible, you are seldom the best of parents or children of parents. If your work is not good and involves practices you personally cannot accept, the stress will kill you. Believe it or not, but the family cannot build such stress within you. You need to live, but work is often the source of your death, so we concentrate on work as the way to begin correcting your life at home.

The only time you feel great is when work and home life are in sync. If you make much money and no one at home cares, you do not enjoy the fruits of your labor as much as you otherwise might. If your family is excited over your advancement, you feel like e the happiest person on Earth—and maybe you are. We want you to enjoy being you and being with your family, but there is time for that only when you finish your spiritual work.

Women work at several jobs and do most of them well, but men may not be so lucky. Often men work at jobs for which they are ill-suited, in order to feed and clothe their families. The family must recognize this sacrifice. If women do not notice it, children are unlikely to notice it.

Whatever your life is now, it can be better. You have a lot of chores left undone. You are not up-to-date on anything. We know. We see you neglect bills when the day is pleasant. We watch you run around shopping when it is bad. You run and play more than work today. Wherever you are, you need time to enjoy yourself, but it takes less time to do it. Going about in haste is not enjoying life. Work fast, but enjoy slow. You need to enjoy your time here, but do not need a lot of time to enjoy yourself.

The response you seek from life is always there. It is in the pores of your body and living within you. All you need do is exercise your right to be *you* and you are.

If your life is drab and dull, work hard to improve it now. We want you to enter into life with a reverence you seldom experience for anything except other people. Stop looking at others and blaming them for their success, instead look at your life and get busy working on it.

You have all you need to be the best you can be!

You need not feel satisfied when your life closes in with only a few years left on Earth—and you are assured you will enter the next plane. You are still here! You must work, too. No one is immune from the need and ability to work as long as your body functions reasonably well. In fact, the body will outlast you if *you* keep it busy.

What about all who do not work hard? Why do you care? You know not who *you* are, so how can you know if they work hard or not? Sit and develop your mental muscles for a week and see if it is not hard work. You may believe you are best equipped for this world because you work with your body, but your mind is also a muscle. It must be exercised and developed by much use.

In order to circulate and meet men, some women are inclined to ignore their inner life in favor of the outer one. However, men are likely to favor a woman who is developed internally as well as externally. Children must be equipped with internal goals and abilities to meet them, if you wish to help them achieve a lifetime of happiness.

You are never without the need to exercise the mind, but the mind can exercise best while you work with your body. We are unable to identify all the areas of an individual's life where there are leaks of energy, but you can easily do that. Simply place your mind in a meditative state and feel the loss. You need not dwell on loss, but you should take steps to identify and remove it.

We will not help anyone unable to identify losses, because we cannot dwell on anyone in particular. Your Guides are here to help you personally. You need their assistance—not ours when your life is not flowing smoothly. *The Holy Spirit*, after all, is the most important aspect of your physical existence. We assume you know that, but we still like to remind you.

Why would you read only horror stories and ugly accounts of murder and mayhem when your mind absorbs such stuff as fact? You can paint over ugliness, but it is easier to keep the mind clean in the first place. Why ignore beauty for ugliness?

In the work of a few is the money of many. You may be helping perpetrate evil by buying stolen work and goods. You need to remind yourself of the person who actually made the product—and those who sustained the loss. Are you willing to look them in the eye and say, *"I don't care if you made nothing for your labor. I don't care if you feel violated because you were robbed!"* You do this when you buy patented work, copyrighted work, or any other hand-produced item from someone who stole it. You, too, are a thief! No excuses are recommended or accepted. Do not continue to do it, if you want to leave when the time comes to ascend.

In the work of a few is the money of those who would like to work, but cannot. If you work and save your money, it may need to be invested. Where do you place your investments now? We suggest you do not know the people to whom you entrust your hard-earned money. If you do not know them, we suggest you may be easily robbed. Know exactly who you entrust with your money. Detail why you are lending them any amount; when you expect to reclaim it; and how much you expect them to pay you for lending it. If this is impossible, you risk all you have.

To invest in you is always the best investment. The next best thing is to invest in your family—then friends, and then the community in which you now live. To invest in worlds where you are not actively living is a way of promoting ego and seldom works well.

We would like the work of your hands to remain after you are gone. We know you do not think much of building monuments, but we would like your home to remain at least for another generation. Why build a home and sell it to the first high bid? You lived your life in the house and can easily afford to give it away, so do not sell it just to make money—unless forced to do so.

There is always a glade in the center of the forest where animals meet and greet one another, but in the center of most towns today there is no place to amble about and act like people. You need to develop enough space within each neighborhood where people can be acknowledged and greeted as human beings. If you do this, you can keep all you have and not be afraid others will steal it from you.

People are not thieves by nature. They learn this from watching others get away with it. Your life will not develop without first watching others live. To watch others enjoy the company of one another is the first social instinct to be followed. You like to enjoy yourself. If you steal, you saw it done at home first. If you like people, you saw it at home. If you like people and can steal from them, you need to be locked up for a short time.

When your mind needs to be relieved of sorrow, you do not seek an enemy. If you have no friends, you go to someone you trust. If you trust no one, you will go mad with sorrow. We cannot drain sorrow from us. We need someone else to help. Be sure you have someone who cares or can be trusted—just in case. How can you be sure of having such a person? Be one!

Welcome to the work of being human. You need never fear. You need never be stolen from again. You need not be alone. You are the sole decider of it all. We will now help you deceive others never again and not be deceived yourself. Once you know where you stand within, you can help others see you as you are. It is your life. Make sure others recognize you exist and are worthy of their trust.

EXERCISES IN BEING HUMAN

1. Keep your eye on the ball! You know what we mean. Visualize it, but if feeling less than anxious to learn about yourself, you will resent it or act negatively now. If you resent a command, you are not acting in your best interests. If you are to be a citizen, you must be part of a community. To be a citizen requires a life of work and determination. You cannot rob, beg, and behave like an animal if you expect to one day be accepted and respected by humanity.

   Put your mind at ease. This is less a statement than a request. Did that seem less stressful? We want you to build a reserve of good will in order to avoid ever acting out in rage. Most of your early years you are full of rage, but it need not be. You can own your life. No one else wants it. Be yourself, no one else cares. But act your age, because everyone is watching to see if you can be socialized or not. If you act your age, few will notice anything else. It is easier to achieve the freedom of adulthood by acting like others of similar age.

2. Put your feet on the floor and imagine you do not know who is in your body. Can you see anyone there? Do you feel anyone else? It would be most unusual if your imagination could furnish you with that sort of image, but if you can visualize such a thing, you run the danger of believing in anything. This could be very harmful to *you*. You must not believe everything the mind conjures.

3. Put your hand on your other arm and grip it to prevent movement, then pretend to struggle with yourself. Do you have the strength to keep your arm from moving? You need to be strong enough to stay erect and be able to protect yourself. If you are frail and weak, you need to develop your body. We will help.

   Your body is not to be built up to impress others. Only a fool wastes his life trying to impress others. Do it for you alone! If your body is not in great shape, it invites others to take advantage of you. Please do not let that happen.

4. Put another's foot in your hand and see if you can lift that one. If you can, you are in good shape. If you cannot, begin lifting

weights to develop strength you need if you are ever in danger from such a person.

5. Place a mirror on the wall and look at your body, but not your head. Do you look great? Shame on you if you said, *'yes!'* Such immodesty is unbecoming and puts off other people. Look at your life as seen through your body. Does it look its age? If it looks younger—great, but do not fret if it looks its age. Worry only if your body looks older than others your age. This is the first sign of aging which reveals the inner you. Be careful to advance at the same stage as your mind.

6. Continue looking in the mirror, but include your head this time. Look at your eyes. Do your eyes reflect light? Look at your pupils and see if you see *you*. If your eyes are a light color, they reflect back more of the world and less of you than dark eyes. You need to let the world know more of you if your eyes are light. If your eyes are dark, you need to watch the world more.

These are only the basics, because you know the rest. You are an expert on you. You live in *you* every day of your life. Sit in the light and see your world. You are there and we are above looking at you through layers of ether, but we can still see only one thing at a time. Be sure to look at your life as a whole and work at it one thing at a time.

Whenever your workday is over, your work on self begins in earnest. Do not sit on a couch or chair in your room and do nothing. Thinking is the best work to do then, but you can read or write and still develop your mind. We will help you develop your mind and body by inspiring you at times when your mind is at rest.

We enter your dreams—day or night, and occupy your ideas, but we cannot enter *you*—nor can your Spiritual Guides. Some humans are so afraid of others entering them that they refuse to relax or meditate. Who would want to enter you? You are not the greatest living organism! You are fine, but you are not great. Get any ideas to the contrary out of your imagination now and get to work. Your imagination is a source of many ideas, and most are connected to your inner self. If you have any fearsome or ugly ideas, reflect back on when you thought such things and remove them.

We will again reflect upon the nature of humans versus others who live on your planet. You need to be concerned about other humans, but are respected for taking care of all others, too. To ignore the life of animals and other living organisms is not worthy of Godly people. If you are Godly, be sure you make everyone aware of it by never treating anyone unkindly.

As you greet the dawn, welcome the new day that lies before you. Do not laze about waiting for others to knock on your door. You are the only one who cares if you live and have a good life—others must take care of themselves while here. While on Earth, enjoy all that is here, but be ready to advance to the next plane where all is so much better.

Chapter **Fifteen**

You still have many things to learn,
This is not the time to begin a new relationship!

First, visualize placing your life at the bottom of a barrel. How much of the barrel does it fill? If it barely covers the bottom, you are too shallow to know love and be able to accept what it means. It is not easy to love—and it is not easy to accept love! However, before you can be *you*, you have to love. Before you can love, you need to know who *you* are.

Second, you must be able to remember the good in others, rather than the evil you believe they intended. Many cannot dwell on the positive, instead live lives full of negativity. You cannot grow in any relationship if you mistrust the other party *at all*. You need to trust in order to always love. When an event occurs where the other party is placed in a compromising position and acts foolishly, you will have a difficult time. If you have no basis of trust to begin with, the relationship will fold.

Third, you need to think for yourself. If you cannot, you live someone else's life. If this is the best life for you—and it is intended to be, you need to know why you are as you are before you can determine who will last in your life. To guess at this is foolish beyond belief. You will find many never liked you who acted as if they did. You will discover some who never cared what you did and still like you.

You will locate old friends all your life, but never know it then. Think before you leap to fantastic conclusions about an old friend. You may have an instant attraction, but probably not going to remember why. Once you have your life in order, old and new friends enter and leave your life. Some could be described as *soul mates*, but most are just old friends from other times.

If you find a friend and believe he or she is your *soul mate*, think about what happened to drive you apart. Why would you split from someone who was perfect? That is not likely. You would not split if you loved each other. You came to Earth to learn how to live as a human being in a very negative atmosphere.

We are also here to help those who wish to leave this planet at the end of this life episode. If neither applies to you, why are you drawn to this material now? *You know why*—that is why!

If the world behaved as you do, would it be a better place? We know you think you have the best life possible, but you act like it is not. Why would anyone act like it was not good to be alive? You often repeat such idiotic statements as: *"I wish I was dead. I wish I could die. I think I'm going to die if I don't _____,"* and other foolishness. You need to believe in life if you are to live well.

If you introduce false ideas to your mind, it will act upon them as though they are facts. You must never say negative things about *you* or you will live to regret it. Putting false ideas into your own mind is bad, but to do it to others is evil. You will be expected to make retribution for all evil you delivered to others. If it amounts to a great deal, you may have to come back and relive this life. We suggest you do no evil now, so you never come back.

What you need to know in order to live with another is why *you* want to live with that person, not why they would want to live with you. If your life is dissatisfactory, living in another household will not clear your path. You have to be certain where you are headed before you get out of the path you are in now. If you try to load your problems onto someone else's life and let them pull you along, you will most certainly regret it. When your life is in order, do not seek to put someone else's life in order. If you do, your life will quickly fall into splinters.

You are not here to order others about, You are here to follow orders!

Whatever you do in life is your decision, and you cannot accept the blame for anyone else's decision that did not work out for them. Obviously, you will never blame anyone for your mistakes, but many try to heap guilt on others in order to manipulate and order them into service. You will not accept such guilt and be manipulated to do what you do not want to do.

If your parents are strict, you are considered to be underpinned by strong people. But if your parents care little about your life objectives, you are not at all underpinned. You have nothing to war against, and probably cannot decide where to go once you leave the parental home. This is not to be condoned. It must be changed.

To bear children is a deep and lasting obligation of the soul. You will be unable to avoid it. Your soul requires you to live and mate. If you never had children in all your lives on Earth, you will be asked to do so now. You are not the only ones trying to enter the next plane without ever having had children, but you will be the first to be returned to an unsafe place to have them later.

To believe you *cannot* raise a child, but can be happily married, is pure rubbish. You either can raise a child or you cannot be happily married. It is that simple. You cannot raise a child and have no sense of why you wanted a child in the first place. If you were robbed of your innocence. It is not a crime to abort such a child, since you cannot assume parental responsibility, but all others who seek to mate and then abort in order to be free of work will suffer for it—married or not.

Suffering does not come from God. God is not who causes your problems or is interested in why you caused them. You are the sole possessor of your life and can clear your life at any moment. It is your right and privilege to live here, but you have to live or be the cause of your death.

No one cares if you die. They only care about their lives and how the absence of one they invested so much love into has been taken away from them. You are exactly the same. Your life here is not the end of the line for you. It is not even the beginning of a whole new life. It is just a stop on the line. You will know so much more once you leave Earth.

We are not here to reveal all the secrets of your past—so do not reveal your nature to all here. Be cool about telling your life story. We know you like to talk—and talk about yourselves, but why not talk about the present and what you are doing now rather than the past and what is of no use to the future?

Work is never finished, but life goes into different stages of development and your work changes. When you change your life, you change your work. You do not necessarily change your life because you change your work. We would appreciate prior knowledge of a change in jobs in order to be able to give advice on the subject, but it is your decision always to enter any new phase on Earth. You may suspect from time-to-time that you moved too slowly or quickly in making a decision, but you seldom realize you made that decision—not us or any other entity.

What you do in your lifetime on Earth is not important, but the outcome of your life is why you came here. Be sure you accomplish your life's goal. If you do not, you are never respected. You have to then relive your life and earn the respect of others. Work is not the basis of respect, but respect never comes to those who do not work.

When you work, or how you work, is of great importance to the soul. If you surround yourself with coarse and ugly circumstances and people, your soul is diminished. You have a hard time recognizing your worth and may even come to hate yourself. We suggest you think of all the people you know, then invite them to watch you at your job. Would you make them smile and feel happy? If you are ashamed to let your friends and family watch you work, how can you advance?

A worthwhile family is an asset, but many have risen above the worst sorts of backgrounds. It is your decision to join in or fight it. You are the only one who cares about what happens to you! You have to decide as early as possible in life if you are to enjoy life or not—then seek the top. Your top will not be like anyone else's, but you can reach it. You only have to plan and work toward your final goal.

What your family does for you is a matter of pride. You could let them do everything—or nothing. It would be wise to be somewhere in-between either extreme if you are to learn important behavioral skills when living with others. If your family is unable to give you material goods, you can one day lend them such. It is how the world works. But if your family gives you nothing spiritual, you will never repay them. We want you to begin to know your family is now *you* in a different way, yet exactly like *you* in many ways.

Live in the shadow or live in the sun, but live!

Whatever you think of yourself, the world will think less of you— but so what? We know you are not as bad as what some might say, but being so concerned about others' opinions that you might try to live your life in accordance with their ideas, in order to please them and be liked, is not wise. Why? Their opinion is not long lasting, but your life is. You will remain here on Earth until you learn to be *you*. Living for others is hardly the way to learn who *you* are.

In the weeks ahead, listen to your mouth talk. It sometimes has a life of its own. Listen to the remarks it makes. Listen to the intent of those remarks. Are you angry, jealous, envious, or covetous of others' material aspects? You reveal yourself every time you open your mouth and talk without thinking. Listen and know you cannot hide *you*.

Who you are and why you are here are two entirely different things. You may think that if you knew why you were here, you would know who you are now, but the reverse is true. You need to remember your life is to be lived by you—not by another. If you get that down pat, you will discover others who succeed are doing the same thing, too.

Welcome all to the dawn of the New Age. If you are unhappy, why would anyone want to join you? We are here to bring joy and hope, but so many working in the spiritual world that is opening today to common people are stuck in old, negative ways of expressing themselves. Open your mouth, smile, and be glad.

Hope is not negativity in a new dress. Hope is love, happiness, and a positive life. Be happy…and hope is there.

Work comes to those who look for it, but it can grow to fill your time if you do not control it. Do all you can in one day—then sleep. You do not have to constantly work. What you do is not as important as being *you,* and your attitude toward it. We would suspect most of you do not like *you,* because you labor at work you hate. Why would you do that to someone you love? No way! Would you take work in order to embarrass yourself? We doubt that very much. You do work you want to do, so act like it!

If you say one thing and do another,
What do you want?

Are you afraid others think you are not a *good* person? Who cares if you are good, as long as you do no evil. We know of many who speak well and act with evil intentions. They will have a high price to pay, but no one knows except those who already know the truth.

Be sure you listen to the message rather than the words of other people. Sincerity is most important. If you can detect a lack of sincerity, you detect a liar. Liars are not to be trusted. If you trust them, you are the fool.

How do you know if the one you love is lying to you? We expect you not to know. Why would you love a liar? You set yourself up for a troubled life if you meet, greet, and live with liars. You would then need no hell after this life.

If your love comes to you in tears and tells you of a lie, you must forget it. If your love denies what you know is true, you must not forget it. Life is to be lived and learned from, but it is not always easy to guess the motives of others. Liars are a special challenge.

Your life has many places where you have freely added or subtracted from words you spoke or actions you took, yet you expect everyone else to be true blue (or whatever you say). Why? Others in your life are shades of *you*. If you are blue, so are they.

What you need to know about another is simple: Will this person help or hurt me? You never know anyone until you spend time alone with them. If you never spend time alone, how will you know anyone else? Some are so afraid of living alone that they marry for no other reason. Why? If you cannot live by yourself, who can help you? If you made that mistake, no one but you may teach that lesson to others.

To divorce because you made a mistake is not as bad as to not divorce when the other person is unwilling to be in your life and wants you to become another personality. If you run away from you, you never lose yourself. If you lived and learned, end the marriage amicably and you both will live easily again within a short time—otherwise, you both suffer long after love is gone.

Putting your life in order first may take years, but it need not. You should not wait until you are middle-aged to marry, since it takes years to learn to live together—and you would be too old to have children by the time you truly knew each other and were ready to rear them together. To marry before the body matures is also a very large liability—especially to the woman. Her health will not be enhanced by having a child before she has stopped growing and learned to care for her own needs.

Working on self in the time left after your labor is over is not enough. If your soul aches, you must seek solace and comfort during the day, but it can wait if you feel joyful. We often see you labor with life—not knowing who you are, and we wonder why you do not sit down and think about it. Why think about work, but ignore *you*?

For the time to come, we have been able to plan a lot of work for you to do, but it is your decision whether or not you intend to continue these studies. If you decide you know enough, you will still grow—but not fast or far. We want you to continue to grow quickly and become accustomed to change.

Change is the modus operandi of the universe

If you cannot change while here on Earth, how do you think you will live eternally? Life is never stagnant. Life is the living of each moment. You need to live if you are to grow. What you ignore will grow even if you do not care for it, but what you cultivate grows more.

The only time in life to be content is when you are dying and have nothing else to do. Until that day, you are here to work on the pace and life you want to display to The Guides the day you cross over to the next plane—if you get to do that. Why would anyone live a life and never cross over? You know why.

You will not cross over to the next plane if you must repeat this life. If you have sinned against your immortal soul or God, it is not to be. You will never exist again if you sin against God, but you can recover if your sins are merely against others you did not recognize as being against you, too.

Blasphemy is the worst sin. You cannot hate God or even say you do without being in danger of harming or destroying your soul. Sound melodramatic? You should see the souls who have done it before you.

Are you now ready to believe? Hardly! Fear is not the way to win souls to God. God created all souls, so how can anyone on Earth return to God? That is idle worship (pun intended). You are not to let others ruin you and your life. If you do, it is still your life and you will pay for it—not another.

We have a few exercises which can help you understand why others are not as clear about you as you think they are. We will help you identify what holds you back in your relationships and spiritually hinders your progress.

EXERCISES IN CLARITY OF THOUGHT

1. DIRECT YOUR EYES TO STAY ON THIS LINE AS YOU CONTINUE TO READ: I AM UNABLE TO UNDERSTAND WHY I AM UNHAPPY? I AM UNABLE TO BE ME. I HAVE NO ONE WHO UNDERSTANDS ME. IF I AM NOT ME, WHO AM I?

   Do not let your eyes move from the top line. You can see the bottom line, too, but may not be able to read it easily. If you can see words below it, but cannot read them, your vision is narrow and confined. If you can read all of it without moving your eyes, you are broad-minded.

2. Center your vision through one eye in the middle of your forehead. Looking out, do you tend to look up or down? Concentrate on looking up. This is how the act of *'Meditating on the Third Eye'* causes thoughts to rise.

   Put your mind *within your mind* and imagine you are captain of a team of nine people. Command each to do their best thing. They cannot help each other. They have to excel at their aspect of what is actually your personality—get them to work together. Are they smiling? Fine! That means you have it all together. If their faces reflect any other emotion, work to change to smiles.

3. Using a list of names you developed from your personal mailing list, cross off anyone you do not *really* know. If you *really* know them, put a star beside their names. Do you have more names crossed off than starred? If so, you are fooling yourself into thinking you have many friends. Friends are not unknown quantities. They are little bits of *you*. If you have no friends, you are unable to help *you* advance.

4. If this list is incomplete after several attempts to list everyone you correspond with, you are inundated with others and need to wean yourself of the need to be surrounded by people. You cannot be yourself if you have no friends—only acquaintances.

5. Using the foreground of any picture, watch it grow larger as the background blurs. The foreground represents the present and the background is the past. Let your past gradually fade out of the picture, and let your work stand out in the forefront now.

6. Write the names of friends on slips of paper and place the paper in a bowl. Every time you need advice, pull a name out of the bowl and talk to that person. If you receive no good advice, talk to *you* about it, then remove that slip from the bowl. Once you have only a few names left in the bowl, you know who you can count on for help if ever needed.
7. Put your life in order before you advise friends on how to put their lives in order. If a friend asks you for help, give what you can, but do not offer more than they asked for—it is not wanted.

When you act as though you have all you need, we never know if you would like more exercises. We find it works well to act confident about how well work is going, so advise you to do the same with your work. You will notice it helps you, too.

We end this chapter with the following advice: Work first on ending your work, then go back to the beginning. If you know how it will end, you know how to proceed from start-to-finish—and that is life!

Chapter **Sixteen**

The only work of this world never done is that which harms you or someone else. You cannot contain evil, but you can refuse to help it grow. The relationship between good and evil cannot be described, but we will work out a way for you to determine if your life is evil or good now.

You are the judge. You either live in the light or live in the dark. It is your decision. For things to grow, you need plenty of light. But to grow wild, you do not need to be cultivated, weeded, or anything that would trammel your roots or boughs. We know you like to grow wild, but that is no longer possible since there are so many souls living together now. You have to let your wildness rest until another time.

For you to grow and gain stature, you need the advice of wise people and whatever else helps you. If you seek advice from fools, you are in danger of getting foolish advice. Be careful of any advisor you ask for help on spiritual matters. If your advisor is left here at the end of life, how can that advisor's followers gain access to the next plane?

If you believe in God, you believe in that which is. You do not know why, or who, or what, but you believe there is meaning to everything you are. The faithless believe they are here to do something well and then leave. Leave for where? This life is not a final destination. *It is the way.* You will hear many people offer many explanations, but it is impossible to know all now.

When you fear you cannot grow or prosper, you attack others. You may attack The Church, the society in which you live, or even your family, but it is not their fault you fear. It is your life, and you must be held responsible for it. If you believe you are a wrongdoer, do you continue doing it? When an evil wrongdoer gets caught, usually the first thing said is: *"I didn't do it!"* What would you say?

If your life were held up to the light and seen as scarred and ugly, would you want the light turned off? Of course, you would. Instead, let the light stay on and study all the lines and scars of your life, then ask yourself why you chose such a tangled path. Ask why you chose to be scarred time-and-time again. Ask why you cannot know if you are doing wrong to *you*. Once you know, then decrease the intensity of the light, but keep it on.

To fall out of the way of God is not the end of the world, but it could be the end of your life. You need to reenter the world and become new again. Once this *'rebirth'* occurs, you can remind yourself of the past, if the past reappears—otherwise, forget it. We will not let you grow out of the past until you know why it was that way. Once you know, you will never be troubled by it again.

There are many in the world who cannot do much about their lives—or so they say. We know of no one who cannot improve! We know of no one tied to another, thus cannot change. We know of not one situation where there is absolutely no good in it.

Simply admit you have to go and then leave. You do not have to argue or fight. People will not bother *you*. If you try to persuade others, you get an argument, but not if you let them alone.

When the day is over and you cannot sit still, think about why you are so agitated. Is it because you never revealed your thoughts, or were you neglected by those in authority? We cannot help you gain the attention of the world, but we can help you gain the attention of the higher planes where you will be living for all eternity—unless you completely derail while here.

You are promised the ability to be able to leave Earth and transcend this plane at the end of a life, but it is your decision whether or not you will do it. We know of no one who cannot help, but we know of many who refuse to work or help. Who would you promote?

Because of the rule set down by God that all humans must be permitted to design their own lives and are allowed to live exactly as they planned, the world is unlike the upper plane now. We know some believe your life is predestined, while others fear it cannot possibly be true. You have a lot of work to do on Earth. You arranged for this life on Earth. You chose your life and parental home. You chose to be born, but you are not held here. You can leave Earth before you are meant to cross over to the next plane. Everything is your decision now.

Would you say you are predestined? You can always decide whether or not you will change. It is always your decision.

The decision to work for evil is the worst intention you will ever make, and *you* will suffer as a result. You cannot work evil. You cannot intend to do evil. You can do things that harm another, but you will pay dearly for it. No one has the power to directly influence another, or cause evil to be done to another without paying a steep price. The old ways of cursing people are still practiced by some evil-intentioned humans, and it still causes them to return to Earth and relive that life.

If you ever worked evil or tried to interfere spiritually with anyone's mind, it is now impossible to return to Earth. The curse of the devil is a stupid idea and was rejected by most believers long before the Christian faith revived it. For some it continues to hold an attraction from the old, old ages. We will not let such foolishness be promulgated or announced as though it were a valid issue to be discussed. If you speak of demons and devils, you do not know of what you speak!

God had a lot of time to prepare you to be here. Your body is not the afterthought of a cold, unrelenting demon or devil. It is the creation of a spiritual being so far beyond your comprehension that you cannot imagine how you were originally created. If you cannot imagine the creation of your body, how could you deal with the creation of your soul?

To dream of a life in which you are pursued by devils and dwarfs in hideous garb is from the vast imagination of a demented soul gone awry. You do not have to believe in God, but you better not believe in a demon of such great power that God is second to it. If you do, you will pay with your soul and never live again.

Every few decades on Earth, someone comes along who has the ability to scream and shriek and be heard over all others who preach sanely and with modulated voices. Why does this noise offer any one solace or cause people to respect their message? You should know by now that those who are losing an argument scream the loudest.

Your life is a record of the times you lived on Earth. You carry memory traces of each time—and you are aware of the times you were here. If you doubt this, place a pillow on your bed as a signal for *you* to go to sleep and let your mind leave your body. Once you can do this easily, you can travel and retrace old past episodes, even venture to explore new or future ones, if you so desire.

We never encourage *'past life regression'*, because it deals only with a person's past and has little present use. If you become obsessed with the past, you stop demanding work in the present and your future becomes clogged in the pipe now leading to *you*—not an actual pipe, but a line of communication that resembles one.

If your life is uncomfortable now, you need only rearrange it until it is comfortable. Never a big deal to do this. Simply try a few alterations, and if major work is required, do it. However, do not try to rearrange others' lives. Attempting to rearrange the life of another person is like trying to work *magic.* You are not permitted to do such evil to another.

Remember: It is evil to try to rearrange other's lives

In the beginning of your present world you called up souls who lived before and wanted Earth to advance. Now you call souls who do not wish Earth to advance—and call it *Satan. Satan* is not a *'prince of darkness'* or anything you were told by well-meaning, but ill-informed persons. *Satan* is a term used by some to denote the difference between those who worship God and those who worship the world.

The world is described as a place where erotic dreams can come true—and elegant men and women can live all their dreams. You do not live in a dream. You live in a world of your own construction. If you do not believe that—you are homeless and have no place in the work of God. Man is not going to create a home for you. Please dream of constructive things to do with your life—and plan to enjoy it.

If you dream and plan destructive works meant to harm another, you will end up in the trash. You may decide to unload your venom onto another, but it would be most foolish to attempt to do such a thing, since you will get it back—doubled. To wish evil is to demean the soul of another, and that other was the ability to ward off evil and command it be returned to the sender. If you send out evil and it is immediately sent back to you, you could end up dead before your time.

There have been people within the deep recesses of time who thought they had power. Those people are still in their former selves. They have not achieved further degrees of education or been able to advance. They will never achieve much, regardless of what they try to do, until they admit they were wrong and want to do right now. If you are such a person and have not had any success this life, repent now and live the rest of your life as a God-fearing individual. You may then be freed of the burden of having to return to Earth.

Life on Earth is not the same as living in the world. The world is a big company of people who are here to live as one. If you think you live in a small town, you know not what you are doing here. If you think you are an American or Frenchman, or whatever, before you can advance to the next plane you must learn to adjust to becoming a human being who happens to live on Earth.

Many of the people who live on Earth are not really human beings. Why would that upset you? You do not know who you are? We do. We can tell angelic beings from humans, and we can tell humanoid beings from drastic things created by thought form in order to create havoc.

You cannot create such things, but we can. Anyone from the upper planes has the ability to create humanoids—but not humans. Only God creates human beings with full capacity to develop and become all they are to be.

If this is too difficult to accept, think of all the computers you created. Not one has the capacity to give birth. It will never happen. You can create robots that look like living beings, but are far from it. We can do that, too, but are much better at such attempts. We are now preparing you for the next plane. We are not here to develop a race of humanoids, but we could.

You are not the oldest beings on Earth. You do not have any of the characteristics of the wise, but you are human and must be respected. Your eldest people are not wise, nor will your youngest ever be wise, but the eldest could become wise if they chose to dedicate themselves to God. It is a path that opens to everyone once—and then closes. If you missed that path, you cannot enter the teaching work we are here to help develop, but you can still be enlightened and reach the next plane.

To develop your life to the fullest is unlike anything you are expected to do. You are expected to develop and experience many things while living on Earth, but few are expectant. As a result, they merely live the same life everyone nearby lives. We are surprised you would do that with your life, *but it is your life.* We cannot help you if you wait until the elders of your community decide if it is all right for you to study. You will have missed your time by then. You need to make your own decisions as soon as possible.

Priests and priestesses are the same. It takes nothing to become a priest in your churches, but to be a priest or priestess of God requires the life of the world be abandoned, and whoever caused you problems must be exonerated. This is such a huge expectation that few ever attempt to reach that realm, but it still exists.

In the churches of your world each *man* had a particular dream of being the center of a congregation of people and achieving his own sort of kingdom—and each woman who formed a congregation hoped to achieve a family. As far as the worlds above and below are concerned, it is the same. You are egotists seeking to form ego-driven societies in which you cannot forget you are human—and do not care to forget it.

To demonstrate how men differ from women in their practices, we could select single individuals and match one against the other, but it is not as well understood as if we compare one sex against the other.

You have two sexes. Some think they do not fit in the one they originally chose—and have trouble with it, but most agree to whatever sex they chose before coming to Earth. To delve deeply into the reason you chose one sex over another takes much time, but it will be clarified in a later volume. We will only say here that one sex has as much to gain from the other as the other does. Both are here for the advancement of the soul. One sex does *not* have an advantage over the other as some religions are prone to promulgate.

If you believe you came to Earth as a man in order to be the more powerful sex, guess again. You came to Earth as a man in order to learn how to prepare for the work of this world. You may have earned less, been a slacker, or never worked in previous lives, so you decided to work in this one. Any man who does not understand from the start that he came to Earth to work is looked upon by all as stupid or misshaped by his family.

If you believe you came to Earth as a woman in order to learn to act helpless and constrained by the rules of man, you are totally wrong. You came to Earth to learn creativity and the ruling of passion over reason. If you do not love or let your creative work flow, you will be consumed with jealousy and hatred. You will learn to defy all who strain to confine you in any way. You enjoy helping the work of God go forth more than men—and usually are more spiritual. However, if a man is spiritual, he will grow more rapidly and root deeper than the average woman.

Now that we have caused you to wonder about why you came to Earth as a man or woman, we can begin to make you question the race you chose. Why would anyone risk coming to Earth as a black or brown individual? To learn humility! However, the risk is great that such an individual will learn to accept the debasing given in large doses by other races. Your race does not entitle you to debase anyone of another race—it is a trap set for all here.

You may wonder why some people have large faces or feet and some do not, but such worries are silly and do not amount to anything. You chose a certain tribe to descend from originally, and chose to belong to a certain race, family, and work-world before you came here. These are the basic elements of your family background and cannot be readily changed once here. You would have to earn a lot of money to change the social class you were born into and may still not be accepted by those above you—so why try? You cannot change the color of your skin, but you can hasten it by intermarrying into other races—but why? If you have a problem with the basics of your life, you have a problem now!

To hate your sex, race, family, faith, yourself is not as bad as hating God. All you need do to cause your soul to die is to say such a thing and mean it. You will never have another chance to live.

We are unaware of the depth of depression some of you let yourselves sink into in order to draw others attention to you, but we observe that depression is a sure way to be ignored. You cannot understand that everyone else is also hungry for attention? Look around and notice all the bags of garbage people are willing to publicly extol in order to be heard or mocked. Some care not what is said, if it means they are noticed. This is the tragedy of your world. No one cares, or cares enough, to look at anyone else but themselves. Thus too many are frightened into acts of senseless horror in an attempt to draw attention only to themselves.

Put your wise people in the headlines and do not destroy them for being famous. Put your fools out of their misery. Do not let their venomous ways be recreated. You will then be able to manage once again what seems to be a totally chaotic lifestyle for all people on Earth now.

What you know—and why you do it seldom matches. Why? If you think one way and act another, you produce stress. If you think you know the way back, you should follow it. If your life is not moving into the right channel, you need to find a pilot to steer you into the safe path again. To ignore the light and let your life go down the drain into a sewer to please another is letting the imbecilic mind rise to its highest degree.

If you do not look ahead, your life has many turns and creates much havoc, but you need not seek out another to tell you what you will do in the future. You are the only one who knows. Only you can tell your story. If you ask someone else to tell you about your life, how do you know they are telling you what is likely to happen? You know how much you plan to do. If something sounds far-fetched, you may say it will not happen, but it could happen if you changed your mind and decided to go along with the other person's version of your future. For this reason, you are cautioned to not seek out others to tell you what your future will be. You can be too easily influenced. You may wish to know what you have in mind, but why ask another? Simply meditate and find out for yourself.

To meditate in order to remember the past is a waste of time. If you want to use time effectively, meditate and determine who you are now and where you wish to be in the future. Never ask a question and then not listen to the answer. You will be given an answer to each and every question you ask, but it takes time to get it through to *you* if you never listen.

What you need to do to easily move into this life is sing and dance alone or with others. Music is a lot like meditation. If it is good, you can lose your worries and cares and not remember them when you return to reality, as you know it, or you can learn to dance and develop a new way to exercise the body, but never sing and dance just to sing and dance. It takes too much energy to sing and dance and not enjoy it. We love to watch all who dance, but we love to feel the music's vibrations more.

Now that you have the idea, look at your life. Look at how many choices you have not made to improve yourself. Act now as though you did make those choices and live as the fullest being you can possibly be. You will then be the fullest being you can possibly be!

The difference between you and other people is not vast, or anything to worry about; but if you waste your time thinking about it, you could lose your life on Earth worrying over it. The best way to spend your time here is to enjoy life and let others live as they wish!

We prepared a few exercises to help you better understand yourself. Once you have worked out each exercise and finished them all, meditate before going to the next chapter. If you can listen, we still have plenty to tell you.

EXERCISES IN LEARNING TO BE YOU

1. Focus your mind on the center of your forehead and wait for your *'middle eye'* to open, then clear your throat. Do you feel as if you can sing now? Do you like to sing? We want you to sing about today, last night, or whatever, but sing a song that tells a story about you.

    Does your song sound funny, sad, serious, worried? Why would you hear such emotion? Because you are experiencing your song in your soul now! Believe in *you* and you will sound like a cheerleader. Do not believe in *you*, and you sound forlorn and lost. Change the tone of your song to change who you are now.

2. Place a glass of water on the floor beside you. Whenever you feel you emotionally cannot rise, reach for the glass. Start out saying: *"I am so sad. I lost my best friend and can't get him back. I feel like crying now."* Then say: *"I'm so happy. I feel like running and jumping and shouting for joy. I want to tell the world all about it!"* Finally say: *"I wish I had my own life. If I had my own life now, I believe I could win every game."*

    Did you reach for the glass at any time? Did you have to stop and take a drink? You are saying little, but are asked to react emotionally. Can you do it or are you stalled in a state of suspended emotion? If you wish to be involved with another person, free up your emotions first.

3. If working on a project requiring your total concentration, do you expect everyone else to know you need quiet? Do you feel everyone should stop their lives to help you now? Do you think

you can concentrate better than others and thus do not need any special consideration?

If you expect others to cooperate, you will be disappointed in people most of your life. It is a small thing, but it reflects your attitude toward others. You may not think you are better than others, but it shows when you do. You may not know yourself, but others do. Think of *you* more and more and you will know you are no different than most others.

4. Work on a plan to develop your body. If you are an adult, you are given demerits if your body is like a young person's, but still expected to do the following:
   - Every day sweat!
   - Every day sit still for at least 10-15 minutes.
   - Every day work on the fear of being alone by being alone for a little longer than the day before, until you can easily be alone for a day.
   - Twice a week look at your face and see if it needs anything.
   - Twice a week look at your body to see if it is fat or thin, then adjust the diet to maintain the same weight.
   - Once a month look at your budget and decide what you need to live on for the next month, then act accordingly.
   - Once a year go to the top of a hill or mountain and lay on your back on the ground and let God enter into your mind and soul.

   If you do all this, you can live alone or among many and never lose yourself.

5. Turn to the next page and begin reading about why you do what you do in order to be accepted. If it makes you anxious, meditate until nothing bothers you as you read.

Chapter Seventeen

The only day of the week you are free of work is when you worship God. If you do not worship, you are not free of work. If you do not accept what you were taught, you have to design your own worship, which takes more time to arrange than if you went somewhere else and joined in with others to sing praise to God and thank all who help you live life as well as you are.

To join others in praise does not require a formal organization, but most people automatically organize into states of formal rules and regulations and end up with ritual. It is very human to do that. To absorb another's ideal into your beliefs is difficult, but not unpleasant for most people. You need to believe in the individual who originally organized the group or congregation. If you disbelieve in his/her ways, you should leave and let others worship as they always have. It is your problem—not theirs. Too many feel that if they are disturbed, others should be disturbed, too.

Whatever you do—do it well! If you worship alone, then sing, pray, and have a good time. If you worship with others, be sure to join in with all things related to the worship ceremonies and rituals, and help form other social groupings that enable you to better know your fellow worshippers. If you do less than that, you are not really worshipping—rather merely visiting, not rooted. You need roots to grow spiritually.

If your relationship to 'outsiders' is not good, it is reflected in the respect with which you worship with others. If you do not feel good about yourself, you will not want to be in the presence of others. You need to analyze why you went your way alone. Decide if now is a good time to review and exact a different outcome from your life. Welcome new beliefs, but do not drop one or two and expect to be welcomed at the crossing over.

You have to anchor your life before you begin a search. If you search into the dark regions of your heart and mind with no basis for belief in God, you lose time. You need to develop a sense of self and belief in one who is all. If you do not, you suffer from a feeling of isolation and despair all this life.

We would never ask you to do something that differs from your personal belief in God, but you should remember God does not appear as a man. You are human and believe everything in the universe revolves around you, but we must inform you that humans are unknown to most that exist now. You have the ability to reason and deduce the cause of an event, but you cannot easily cause an event. This is just one small way you are different from most who share the universe with you.

Without God in your life, you will harm others. You will not know God is a feeling of individualism not discernible to the naked eye (so to speak) and not animal or mineral. You have to feel to believe.

If your emotions are blocked or retarded in their growth, you will not know love. Love is the emotion most closely recognized as being of God, but fear has an element of God within it, too. There is a chill or excitement to the flesh that comes from God moving through you, and it is recognizable to most. If you have never felt it so far this life, you must have had a terrible time.

Your life here and now is not the only one you have. You live on several planes with different levels of understanding on each of those planes. As you advance, you merge with yourself until you are a single entity and have only one soul—YOU. At this time you are only one aspect of that entity and experience many different things on various levels of this reality. You could read about it from others who have channeled such material, but many of you would not follow up on your readings, so we will scan your mind and deliver only what you need to comprehend the immensity of the universe to be able to pursue the proper path now.

Your life here on Earth is not your only life, but it is critical that you do all you can to deliver this life in a proper form at the end of this cycle, in order to be admitted to the next plane. The next plane is not *heaven*, even though some of your religions call it that. We expect you to know the heaven you expect is not there, but one day will be replaced by yet another level of that plane—and another, until you are ready to move from that plane to the plane above it.

Your term on Earth is not exactly the easiest phase of your development. No one came here to be placed in another dimension. You came here to work in bodily flesh and exact from it every possible feeling. If you do not have a full life, you have no time to develop your entire being while here. We expect you to dwell in the flesh, and endure the pain and suffering of the flesh, but you should not inflict pain on others.

If you hurt another, you will be repaid in kind. You cannot stir up controversy about another's name or reputation without having it land on you, so do not get involved with those who defame others. Work on what you can do well. If you cannot do something well, keep at it for a while before giving up. Sometimes you are tested to see if you deserve such a great gift.

When you notice another putting out feelers to determine the way you think, be aware they are attempting to deny you your rights. If there is no falseness about them, they will clearly state initially why they want to know your opinion. Do not give away your opinion. If asked for it, think about whether it is needed or not. If it can help, fully give it. If it is merely a phrase another will use to launch a tirade against you or someone else, let the other wait to discover what you think. Never supply ammunition to those who would kill you with it.

What you do to your life here is not necessarily the only life affected; you will be held accountable for all implications of your conduct now. You may decide to kill another and serve the time, and never serve time above. You are to be repaid in kind for all evil you do here; and if you do not repay it while here, the only thing you can do is repay with your soul—which is not the way to help another.

Your life is not to be wasted nor the life of anyone you are responsible for teaching the ways of this life. If you fail to teach your charges how to live properly, you will be held accountable. Teaching is the highest of all professions and requires dedication. If you fail to dedicate your services, you will be mauled by the mood of the times and unable to enter the next plane this time. You best remember why you chose teaching and respond—or get out before the end.

Empty stools are no way for a business to prosper, but many schools are half-empty of students. Why are so many students not in school? Your society is not equipped for all the people it has, because you do not care if some waste their lives. As a society you will be held accountable for such waste.

In the end times, which are quickly approaching now, you will be expected to honor all your commitments to Earth before you can advance to the next plane. If you have not fulfilled your promises, you will be back and may never have a chance to clear Earth. If you do not clear the atmosphere of Earth, you will not survive. **Remember:** You need oxygen and water to live.

Work to cleanse the water and air is beginning now, but too little too late by too few. You must recommend that the air and water be allowed to sit for a generation and not be polluted; however, greed will not permit such wisdom to exist. It will be mocked and derided until Earth is devoid of humans. Other beings can continue to live here, even if humans no longer can exist.

Work on the world you constructed is very slow. You hate change. You cannot work out of your way on *you* now. In the recent past you have lost so much time chasing after false prophets, you now have no great morality.

We see you daily move a monster to the top and then topple that one—only to produce another monster the following day. Why? If your relationship to God is nonexistent, you will never know who is of God and who is not! You will know when such beings blasted into the airways are to be accepted or not, but for now you should avoid such matters. Let no one ever call and ask you for the way. If you give such matters serious consideration, you will be asked further advice and be exposed to even more derision if wrong.

Let others find their way in their own way

When you see others lift their heads and ask for help, do you ask them why? We see many of you are suspicious of others. You do not ask for help and will not give any. Why think others are after something you have? Do you think they intend to steal from you? If you think like that, you must have stolen something.

You reflect back to others what is within your being. If it is in you now, it will travel back to your soul. You cannot help your soul deliver itself up to God if you collect negativity. You need to reflect the positive effects of Earth.

What you do to your body may not affect another, but many are affected by the way you inflict yourself with disease or injury. If you set out to kill yourself, do it with a gun and let others be nowhere near you then. You will condemn your eternal soul, but you will harm no one else. If you take another with you, you will never be allowed to recover—ever.

Some subconsciously decide to hurt themselves by ignoring the warnings of the wise. They are unable to answer for their actions, yet know their actions will endanger others. If such is the case, that person will be expected to recompense others for any lose—and it may take many lifetimes to do that. Be sure you take no one else's health from them.

We are aware you often sit and muse about why you have less material wealth than others—and are sure you cannot gain it. You have the same wealth as all others, but some people are more capable of managing it than others. If you work daily and have nothing left at the end of the week or month, you are wasting your time working there. You need enough money to spread from one pay period to the next. Some of you have enough money, but seemingly cannot spend it wisely. That is the only way we know you can end up poor. Eventually, all others can earn enough money to meet their needs while on Earth.

Whatever your needs, we know you can fulfill them and get what you need, but you act like you have no access to such material. We would remind you that it is you who decided to approach Earth in the socio-economic, racial background you were reared in. In your soul you believed you could make it here. Thus do not say you cannot, because you know within *you* that you can.

What goes into the stomach is not as important as when it goes in and why it goes in. If you eat for nourishment, the poorest of diets will supply you with enough strength to accomplish your tasks. If you eat all you want when you want it, you will grow such a huge body you cannot accomplish what needs to be done. Live like the bird and eat often—but eat lightly.

When your heart is open to the air of the universe, you feel it is open to all beings. If your heart is not beating because you are afraid, how can anything enter you? Work to clear the atmosphere around you and you will enjoy life. If you continue to work or play in a place where you are afraid, all life is impaired.

The only one who wants you to succeed is *you*! No one else cares. You have to decide early in life you are going to succeed—then get in gear. If you wait until late in life to start your work, the days are then too short to accomplish all you need to do in one short lifetime, thus you must return.

This is the only time most of you can be here!

The world is changing and cannot succeed as is. Your life on Earth is not to be remembered, but it has its reason for being. If you think you are at the final stage of evolution, you need help.

The work of this life is for you to become the best of the best human beings. If you seek to be less than that, you will never advance. Some of you deride others and persuade them not to cope with life and instead let this time go, but you will be made to pay for such ignorance and possible evil. No one can harm another intentionally and live without repayment of that debt to Spirit.

You will know why you are here on Earth when you are no longer here, but some can discover that while still here. It takes practice to meditate to such a level that your inner sources can identify you are consciously uncomfortable with the degree of information you found in the *real* world. Once you discover how to meditate that deeply, you can ask such questions and receive valid replies.

If your state of mind is not scattered—and you feel centered, you can channel. It is not a mystical experience, but requires the ability to concentrate. Most people have the ability, but few are dedicated enough to seek out the God of their soul and ask for help developing their spirituality while on this plane. If your state of mind is never centered, you have to seek out others to advance your work. Why ask others to do your work when you need only learn to concentrate and meditate? All who have any sense of themselves can do it.

What you need to know in order to meditate is not what allows you to meditate. It is the determination to succeed that wins the day. You need remember nothing. You have nothing to do. You will not be expected to remember anything when done, and you need not speak of it ever. Meditation is simply taking time to be *you*.

If God of All is here among us, How can you not know it?

Do you not realize your life is no different from that of others? We pity you if you feel that way. You have the same abilities and disabilities as all others, and you are expected to remain as centered as possible all of your lives here in order to keep to the contract. What if you do not have a contract? Everyone does. You make no decisions based on idle curiosity.

You are never assigned to a life. You have nothing on Earth when you enter or leave, so where do you get all the materialistic stuff you carry around with you all this life? You choose it. You are the only one who possesses what you have. No one else cares if you possess anything. If the only time you feel good is when you buy something that no one you know has, you are then feeling very low in Spirit. We would recommend you instead sit and meditate on the many ways you fear others.

Do you need help?
Not if you have a firm belief in God!
Otherwise, Yes!

Depression is not caused completely by you. It comes from not realizing God of your present life is in all beings. You think you are worthless or extraordinary, and all who live on Earth are ordinary and worthless beings. It is your way to build a life based on such beliefs, no other beings in the universe handicap themselves that way.

Work is not the answer to depression, but it can be used to ignore the pain of the wicked who hurt others or depressed them in order to take away their lives. We will help all who work to *discover the way*. If you need to know anything, ask aloud for the information and we will answer you by written or oral communication. It may be different from what you expect, but it will be quick.

To establish your life on Earth you need great enthusiasm and belief that God exists in everything you are, everything you do, and everyone you meet. It is that simple!

Work on the following exercises now, and once you complete each and every one of them—meditate. Do not skip around! If you omit an exercise, you must return to it before going to the next chapter. Meditate between each exercise or risk becoming annoyed by the image that you cannot accept instruction and refuse to meditate.

EXERCISES IN REACHING THE INNER SELF

1. Quietly place your mind within the waves of the ocean and seek solitude. Let your dreams be of the wind and elements. Do not let anyone interrupt you as your mind floats. Let the water flow and the wind blow. Your mind is now free of all the restrictions of this world. When done, open your eyes and look at the space where you are. Is it brighter? Is it good or bad? Is it for you or not? How do you feel? Now let this feeling remain with you as you meditate.

2. Work out a plan and enter it into a book or journal. If the plan is good, sense your hand is unable to change it. If it requires revision, change it without consciously directing your hand to write. Did you write or not? While you remain seated with pen or pencil in hand—ready to write, let your mind enter into a meditative state. If your hand starts to move, let it. Do not edit or erase text. Let your hand write. If you can read what is written, fine. If you cannot, fine. Now meditate to see if your plan is a good one.

3. Find a little place where you can be alone, then sit and stare at your hands. Do you see anything in them that looks evil? Do you see anything ugly? What about the skin looks green, gray, or hideous? Why would you think a witch looks strange? If the word has very negative connotations, why would you call yourself a witch? Are you afraid of *you*? Look deep into your hands now and see if any evil arises from them. How could evil exist within them? Why would you fear body parts? Think straight! Be wise! Meditate on the miracle of your hands and how they work.

4. Put your life in order and let others know you are not yet ready to die, but if you died now you would be ready. Is that a scary thought? To die is accepted as the outcome of life. How can you say you will not die? You know you never die—that is why you say to yourself: *"I'm not going to die"* and mean it. If you say: *"I'm ready to go whenever God wants me,"* you are ready. Think of everyone who will miss you when you are gone. Are there many? Why? Now meditate on becoming more popular.

5. Popularity is not an easy goal. Is it? You have to gain a modicum of knowledge about many different subjects in order to chat with others about non-intellectual matters, yet be intelligent enough to know when to use that information. Do you know who you are? If you do not, it will immediately show up when you start talking. If you initiate the subject of discussion, you will find yourself unable to change it. When you speak and expose yourself to others, you learn something about yourself, but more about *you*. If you wish to meet and learn about others, first listen to them. If you wish to learn about yourself, talk. Sounds odd, does it not? If you sit back and meditate on it, you will know the answer to this riddle.

6. The only work to do on a daily basis is what cannot be done at other times. If it needs to be done today, do it! Letting it go undone will result in future failure. Ask no one to help you with your work. Do it yourself! When you can easily do all of it, look for more. Do not sit and idle the day away, unless you are disabled and cannot physically or mentally take on more work now. Mix your work to make it more interesting, and time yourself to determine how efficient you are. Once you know all this, you can evaluate your worth in the workplace. Once you gather such data, meditate on what work you should do for others in the workplace and for yourself at home.

7. Pull from memory your oldest living relative and envision his or her picture. Do you look like him or her? Do you resemble this person in any way? Why would you? Why would you not? Look into their eyes and see if you can see you there. How could you live within that person, even though you are a direct descendent? You cannot—and no one can descend into you, either. You cannot be overtaken by the spirit of another entity—only your own. You must not fear if another aspect of *you* avails itself in a dream or wakeful state and attempts to interact with you. After all, you are the entity who makes up your soul in only one aspect—and if you can merge now, it will take less time later.

That last exercise is a very difficult assignment for most and requires time to assimilate, so we will not end this chapter here. Instead, look at time. Does it fly or straggle by you?

Work is not good if it takes so much time that you feel it drag. If you are into your spiritual work, you never notice time passing. If the work of the land is unworthy of you, you may not notice time passing, either.

We suggest you look carefully at the work you do and meditate upon why you do it. If you then become uncomfortable, it is because someone deep within *you* hates it and wants you to do something else. You could grow much faster if you let the other *you* end its agony and be allowed to grow into work you are now doing on Earth.

We are now ready to drop this subject, but you are not. Sleep on it and enter notes into your notebook or journal. We assume you keep one!

Chapter Eighteen

You change—not others. If you think someone else is not as they should be, you are who thinks it—not the other, so you must change. You either accept that one as is or change into another personality. You may *not* expect others to conform to you. This is egotism and not to be condoned in anyone—especially you.

Now that the tone is set, let us depart to a neutral area where you can see how much you expect of yourself versus others. You will see the difference is not subtle. You either expect nothing of others and everything of yourself or the reverse.

We would like you to decide to be different. Think about an area of your mind where you often run and hide if others attack you. Does it look like you, or is it dark and crowded with things leftover from the past? Let your mind empty and clear it now. Replace the darkness with bright sunshine. Is that easy to do? You probably cannot do it because you let it remain that way for years, however, it can be cleared.

Let your mind's eye focus on the center of your forehead and begin clearing out all darkness present. Can you do that? If so, you can clear out past darkness, too. If you cannot visualize it, you will be overburdened with ills and disappointments that overshadow your life until you rid yourself of the past.

People who worry constantly usually worry more about themselves than others, but they do spend time thinking about others' problems, too. The way to live is to decide for yourself what you should do, not to decide how another is to live. You will never encounter anyone who is delighted when you tell them how to live their life—so do not do it!

Working on others leaves little time to devote to your inner life, especially if your outer life is hectic. If you devote no time to *you*, using your energies to solve others' problems, you help them explore their life and get beyond this plane—but what about your life here?

Do you think it better to sacrifice than merely help? Never sacrifice your own beliefs for another! You need to believe in life hereafter and recognize you will enter it alone. No one else is going to be there when you leave. Your Spiritual Guides accompany you, but they are not held responsible for your life.

If you think you are wiser than the young, think about it. What wise person sets out to know the answers to all of a child's questions? No one wise does that. You would find yourself totally behind in your work before the youngster was out of adolescence. You need to donate time to the young and keep them from damaging their souls, but you are not to give up your soul for others.

We would never expect you to give up anything for us. We are not your only friends, but we are your best teachers here and now. If you cannot understand us, you can now understand why your friends do not like to hear you teach or preach. It is not pleasant to find out you know nothing. You may fear you are the only one who is ignorant or stupid, but you have many companions on Earth who know nothing, yet are confident they are superior to others. It is a common frailty of human beings!

Measuring yourself against others is not smart to do. You have nothing in common. Believe us, you are all totally different. No one on Earth is close to being the same as you or us. We exist in the same mental framework as you do now, and work inside *you* to develop a better world and life for you and others on Earth.

Most people you meet do not begin to recognize your growth, let alone who you know. To know someone well requires years of dedication and devotion to that single person. We would not recommend you do that since your life here is short—and not long until the next one. You need enough time to develop you before *you* leave. So if you linger and wait on others, you will not finish your work in time. Begin early to understand others, so you can live in peace—but do not live for them.

Men are dedicated to the work they do on Earth—often to such an extent that they totally ignore their families, which is not as bad as not working at all. We know this is a shock to some who just tuned into our message—nevertheless, it is true.

Women are willing to give up their success and dedicate their lives in service to others. If they do that now, many others think them strange or weird, but they achieve great rewards from the planes above for this dedication. To dedicate your life to the good of all is a job—and work is necessary to develop this life. If you never work, you will not develop—thus you cannot pass.

Women and men who marry and raise large families accept the job of building nations. If they do it well, the nation is strong. If they fall down on responsibilities due their children, long before the population at large is aware of it, the nation is in a dire state. If you want a strong nation, you cannot let those who do not like children raise them. You must care for the children or lose the nation.

We weep now for the many children lost and slain each time such a nation is lost. You can never raise them from the dead, but you can stop it from happening again. You need to take time now to evaluate your entire social system.

Do you encourage people to idle and waste their lives? Do you expect some to do work for everyone else? Do you expect some to work all their lives, while others regularly take off work for long periods—especially when young? You must understand why as a people you condone such unwholesome practices.

If you cannot change <u>you</u>,
How can you change the nation?

It is actually easier to change a large group with incorrect thinking than it is to change the mind of one person. You need not engender fear or use terror to change a group's thinking—just infer how adversely others look at them for doing whatever. As a group, most people want to be well thought of by all. As individuals, they will hide behind the group and protest they have no power to change.

What you do with your power to change is not important, but what you change is! If your life is growing deep and downward, you will not recognize the shallowness of another's thinking unless you listen to the reasoning and results of such a person's thinking, actions, and life. You need to listen, but it can be a blinding experience. Be sure you are firmly installed in your belief system before listening to what others think, or without any thought you may start to believe as they do.

Now and then a personality is created that enhances the life of many. This personality exists on a number of different planes and can be instrumental in developing many people in many different ways, but that personality may still be lost. You need to develop into the many ways you are *you*.

If you fear you are being swallowed up by another—leave. If you cannot stand alone and are fearful about what will happen when you leave, stay away. If you can stand and survive, you may reenter another's life without fear of being absorbed into it and thus lost.

What to do if lost in another's life? We would expect you to seek a Guide and find your way out. Who better than the Spiritual Guide assigned to your life while here on Earth and has a vested interest in seeing you advance to the next plane? Who else could be more interested in you? No one, not even us!

You are the result of *reincarnating* (as you say) many times on this planet and others. If you decide to end the process by committing a mortal sin (immortal sin would be a more accurate description), you will end a long line of mental and physical developments for a life of vice and crime against humanity. Is it worth it? Never! You have to live and be able to develop, or you cease to exist.

Your life on Earth is not the best of lives, but it could be worse. You could return to lower levels of this plane and exist as an animal of lesser intelligence or even as plant life. You are surprised? Why? You did not spring from an ape, but you once were one. It is God's way to develop a soul in every aspect and create from within the core of a being the perfect place for all to dwell.

You need to develop your life, since those who went before you did. If you ignore all life within you, you will harm and maim animals and plants, thinking you are their superior—not realizing you are all alike. Animals can be eaten, so can plants, but to cut them up for no good use is egoism and evil. You need to remember they are here to feed and clothe you—not to be sported with. If you kill and destroy in order to gain—you lose.

The only people to know you are those who live with you. Do you know the people you live with now? No, you do not know anyone. You cannot. You can assume many things—and you do, but you cannot know why or how a person thinks the way he or she does. This is a private matter existing only within that individual. You are not expected to reveal your thoughts, and you should never expect others to do so, either.

Psychologists and doctors of psychology and medicine are not the best people to talk to, but some of you have no one else. Is that not the saddest state for a human being to reach? You need help, but where do you go to find it? The term *'psychologist'* does not impart to us any other meaning except the one we read in your dictionaries. How do you read it? Many of you seem to think it is their job to live your life or tell you what to do. How can they do that? It is always your job to live your life!

People adept at other arts and sciences are as evolved as psychologists, but exhibit less interest in people. If you had a problem with your car, would you expect a mechanic to know why it is not working properly? You would. If you your body is not working, can you expect a doctor of medicine to know why? You cannot. God is the creator of your body and God alone knows why it is not working as designed. A mechanic may be able to build a car or truck, but a doctor cannot build a body.

Only a creator or designer can know the causes of stress and strain and how to remedy or rebuild to alleviate problems. Doctors should not be held responsible for being unable to help you when sick. It is your body. You must know why you harmed it or let it fall into disrepair, and learn how to clear it of negativity and acidity to heal it.

Your life on Earth is not over, but you could go at any time. You do not know when. It is better that way so you do not fret. If you knew, what would you do to prolong your life? Nothing can prolong life once the mind and soul decide it is time to leave. Medical personnel today try to keep the body and soul together longer, but it is idleness at its worst. No one wants to live in a body in total disarray or stinking of disease, so why prolong such life? Egotism! You are not to prolong what God has left to the Earth to reclaim.

Many are angry when others do not regard life in the same way they do and protest loudly and constantly to God about abortions and death sentences for criminals. We would ask them to quiet their minds and hearts and acknowledge that many souls cannot live now. So many souls on Earth now have no chance for a decent life here that more are not needed. If a person fears she cannot live and raise a child, you cannot change that mindset with talk, but you can make them sick at heart with guilt and wish to die.

Keeping your opinions to yourself and letting others do the same is much safer for the entire planet. If the world you created is not good, you made it that way and need to change. If the work of the world is no longer good, you need to improve *your* work. If the world is not thinking like you, do *you* know why?

We think some constantly think adversely or contrary because it gives them a certain standing in the community and enhances them in their own eyes, but to resist the flow is not wise. If you live in the middle of a river and cannot bend, you will be broken. You cannot live in the mainstream and expect not to be swept away as time goes on and the water deepens with storms and floods of emotion.

The work of the world is not the work of a single person, but a single person can do much work and live long in the world. It takes only one decision to make you determined to do something new. If that decision is not good for you, then change it immediately. The longer you wait to change, the harder it is to do it. Your age is a determining factor in how easy or difficult it is to change habits. You cannot be *you* if you cannot change, but to change too much is not good for you, either.

When the world does not recognize the work of one person, it will often take notice when several work on the same project. You then have a counterpoint and image on the reverse side. For example, if you work as an artist, there is an artist doing the same work as you—but doing it differently. You can join together to be noticed more.

You will know, as you continue to live, that many people adopt work, because they saw it done well by another. The original work is outstanding, but copies are blurred or unrecognizable as being copies. You must do your work and not copy another. To copy another's work is not the mark of genius, rather the mark of laziness. You have original work within you—do it!

Whether or not you have a great deal of talent, you can do at least one thing well and have the ability to make a living doing it. You may need to experiment and try a number of different work areas, so do not restrict your life by doing the least favorable of your many talents and cause yourself more grief and unhappiness than those less talented. Yes, you cause your own grief. No one—certainly not God—creates grief for any reason other than to learn to develop into the best possible creature within this plane. If you think you learn the hard way, you do. If you think you learn fast or easily, you do. Try it sometime and notice the difference.

Welcome grief, then let it dry before you once again assert your usual life. Grief comes whenever you need to be dependent upon another. It ends with the assertion of the soul. Your soul is not dependent, but you are. If you are never dependent here on Earth, you are not living the life you came here to live. Grief is a necessary part of development here.

Whatever your life is here on Earth, you designed it and now live it. We cannot change you or your life design, but we can help you redesign and retool your body in order to live a life of greater depth and enjoyment. **Remember**: What you do is your decision—no one else's; your Spiritual Guides can only direct and steer, never command.

Some of you ask questions and hear answers you believe come from your spiritual source, but they do not. You cannot expect the truth to come from your ego. It lives in the world and exists to take care of daily work and bodily needs, but it is not the seat of your wisdom. You need to go deeper and find *you* hiding among the brooms and mops in your mental closet. Once you discover how to reach your highest self and ascertain what you need to know, you will not be fooled by the voice of your ego. Until then, you may be operating in the false belief that *'the little voice inside me'* is your inner wisdom when it is not.

Obviously, your inner wisdom is not inner as in inside your body. You need to travel into your mind to find your wisdom. If you feel unsafe or insecure, you cannot travel to *you*. To connect with your inner life, first clear the air around you of all negativity. Violence cannot be condoned, since it is alien to peace. Once you are at peace, you can begin to meditate and seek your inner wisdom.

We have heard that some people are afraid to meditate because of worries instilled in them during their youth by well-intentioned elders who feared they might be *'taken over by something'* if they meditated on their own. You have to understand that many people do not know anything, and if you listen to them, you will never grow. You must learn for yourself all you need to know. If you cannot learn on your own, you will be retarded—by no one but you. The elders of Earth are no longer the wisest, but they are wiser than most of the young.

Working on the ways of the wise is not for everyone. It takes time and energy to develop. If you have little time after your daily work is done to concentrate on your spiritual work, you will not grow as wise as those who work then. You will not be held back if you did not have time due to working so hard and long in the service of others that you had no time for yourself, but you will be held back if you had time and did not develop this life.

Poverty is not the curse you may have been taught to believe. It is not a measure of laziness and sloth. The cure is in neither of those traits. You need to recognize that times change and people do not. Many people enter a field of endeavor and refuse to leave it—even when there is no more work in it. You must find work if the source of your revenue is gone. To idle away your life letting others take care of you when you are not disabled is to set yourself up for a return to work very, very hard the next time.

Poverty may be your curse, but not seen that way by another. Some look upon wealth as a curse, but it is not. Your viewpoint is yours alone. You cannot look at others and expect them to see it as you do, since you live at different levels and develop different aspects. You do not have the same goals. Work for your goals and let others aspire to theirs.

We would expect some of our readers to know the difference between what you think on Earth is right and wrong, but that cannot be. No one on Earth is exactly like another. You all seek different goals and ends to your lives. If you think like us, you are not at all like others. If you do not think like us, you are not at all like others. It makes no difference who or what you are—you are very different from everyone else. Be pleased, but not proud that your life is different. It gives you an opportunity to be *you*.

People who mutilate their bodies and/or dress gaudily in order to attract attention are seldom liked by the average person. Why? Because you immediately recognize their weakness! When they want you to notice them, they appear insecure. Therefore, you reject them and seek those who are more secure.

Working on you in order to impress another rarely, if ever, works. Some people start out trying to impress another and become that person. You must be careful to stay within your life and not become absorbed in another's.

If you lose, listen to your Guides and act accordingly. It is unwise to leave a life so quickly that you feel it. Instead, gradually withdraw from the aura of another and let that person realize you were not there to harm or absorb them, but once so weak in ego that you believed you had to merge with them to live. If you divorce, you do this. We will not let you divorce yourself from *you*.

Do not act like you do not want to be you!

You must accept yourself—and the easiest way is to learn to accept others. If you can do this, you are almost there. Once a person cannot believe in others, how can that individual be sure of self? To believe in self requires a lot of work, but it is not difficult. You can have a lot of fun finding out about *you*, or make life serious and overwhelming— but why? Let your life be happy and have fun! Do not believe it must always be serious. You need contrast to develop fully, and your life is no exception to that rule.

Within the world are many who would like to rule you, but you have to permit that to happen. No one can take over your life! You decide who has the power to control you. If you are wise and have good parents, you will decide early to let them control you while young, but later in life you will explore and determine why you cannot do certain things. If you learn easily, you grow quickly. If you learn best the hard way, by trial and error, you take much longer to become wise.

We would like to see everyone learn much more quickly than you are now, so we suggest parents help by being wise and uncomplicated in their approach to child-rearing. Take care to help, but not complete a child's tasks. Raise them to fear God—but not man. Let them know you care and will be there, but not always. If they know this, you will one day be able to leave them and live your own life again. If you fail to instill this message in your children, they will return and return until they are no longer children but dependent adults. The bane of this world is dependent adults. You need to correct this now!

Within each personality a baby exists. You need to grow and let this baby know it must grow, too. If you permit this infant to control you and your life, you will be unable to absorb the real message of this life and have to return. Some believe you have found this child and now worship it. Why? Why would you worship a child? You are growing constantly and each stage is better than that which preceded it.

Life is not a place to hide, but a place to gain self-knowledge. You cannot remain immature. It is hideous to do that! We will not let anyone who comes to us like this remain a child. We see no need to hinder anyone in order to establish our position. Do you?

Some people are guilty of 'infantizing' another in order to keep them tied to them or dependent. This will result in mutiny when least wanted. Try to let your life be a guide in rearing your children. If you are okay today and fear nothing much, rear your child as you were raised. If you are an emotional mess with so many fears and disbeliefs that you cannot understand why you are here on Earth, then you may decide to reorganize your methods of rearing children and differ from the way you were raised.

Parents are blamed much by misfits, but not by children who grow into healthy, well-adjusted adults—many of whom often praise them. We know if you are one or the other simply by listening to you talk. Are you aware you give yourself away that way? We thought not.

You now need to do a series of exercises. We want them done slowly and deliberately. If you feel a need to rush, leave this work until another session when you have time to develop it. We know you hate to work on difficult areas and often become annoyed with them, but we recognize this as a way to determine your weaknesses. We want you to work hardest on the exercise that annoys you most.

EXERCISES IN SELF-DEVELOPMENT

1. Imagine you are driving along a major highway when you spot a car like yours traveling in the opposite direction. Ask yourself: *"Is that me? Am I over there, too? Could I be going in two different directions now? Why would I be over there, if I am here?"* The answers will surprise you. We know if you try to imagine yourself in two different places you get upset, because you feel stretched, but this is good for you to do. You need to stretch in order to grow to your fullest potential without bursting a seam.

2. If your car stops on this highway, can you feel it? Do you want to immediately start moving again? Do you feel you should check to see if there is a problem? Are you nervous? Are you calm and cool, knowing it is just a minor set-back? Who do you expect to help you: the police (authority), a trucker (professional), another driver (peer), or a parent? You have learned much, but still must learn you need no help, if you know what to do in all instances now. How do you reach that place? You study and work on *you*.

3. Put your life on hold and examine the life of your parent of the same sex. Do you recognize the similarities and differences between you? Are you comfortable with this parent? Do you appreciate this parent as an adult? Do you fear or dislike this parent? Why? Work on this.

4. Imagine asking your parents to give you a gift. Do you like it? Do you pretend to like it? Are you aggravated, because it does not reflect who you are? Why? Do your parents know who you are now? Why? Would you take time off today to explore one aspect of life with your parents? If you cannot do that, you have a serious problem with authority, as well as your parents—regardless of their sex. You must develop some avenue of respect to enter into meaningful conversation with your parent(s) before you can fully embrace adulthood.

5. Which describes you best? You hate to begin projects, but like doing new things once started. You like to start things, but never get around to finishing them. You think people waste their time on hobbies and reading. You think people who do

not read are mental midgets. You hate *'small talk'*. You love to talk. You never sit still. You hate to run around all the time. Your life is settled and secure and you feel at peace, but wish you had more adventures. You are so busy you cannot sleep.

Can you identify others' needs more quickly than you can describe yours? If you said 'yes', your priorities are not in order. Get them in order now! Know God comes first, *you* second, your children (if you have any) third, and all others after that—including us.

6. Assume your life is blooming and growing so fast you cannot express your joy now, so you enter a contest to see if you are the best at what you do. Do you win? Do you lose? Do you see such races as not worth your time? Why would you compete against anyone when you are happy to be *you*?

7. Imagine you hire a band and hold a dance in order to deliver the news about your new body and soul-seeking life. Would you ask everyone you know to attend? Would you ask only family; only friends; all strangers; or only acquaintances and strangers? Why? Who cares if you bloom now? You do! Ask only those who love you. If none love you now, you have a lot of work to do before celebrating your rebirth on Earth.

8. Write each of these lines on a little card:
   I am having a great time!
   I hate what I am doing!
   I want to change!
   I will do something new today!

Every day pull out a card and watch what kind of mood it produces. If you cannot see any change, you are living now, but have to see things before you believe. You feel depressed if you dwell in the past; if living in the future instead of today, you become anxious about anything that produces a negative connotation. Pull out a card that causes you to fear or worry. Look at it and examine why you do not want this card in your life. This is an area that requires intense work now.

Work on all these exercises, but re-evaluate where you stumbled or got angry while completing the task. That identifies areas where you are stuck now.

What you do now determines your life tomorrow, so be sure you do your work today and not let it go until tomorrow when you will have much more to do. We want everyone to enjoy today, but not at the expense of the future. If the past was good—today is good! If the past was filled with bitterness and disappointment, remnants of it are still around today, so ease up and release it.

You can break any chain, but it must be done steadily—one link at a time. Do not sit and work on the rest of your life. Instead, work on *you* and who you are now, because tomorrow is built on today.

Your life here now is the most important piece of business you must accomplish today; but if your business life is left to rust, you will have many mental problems. Control the urge to neglect your family, friends, and elders in order to enjoy only yourself—and you will have a wonderful life!

Chapter **Nineteen**

Whatever your life was up until today, it cannot be changed. Your past is gone forever! Your life today is based upon the past, but exists only *now*. You will build the future upon the actions you take today, but the actions of today may not bear fruit for many years.

Do not forget to think about reactions to your actions. If your life is simple, you think others live simple lives, too, but you are wrong. Most people live very intricate webbings of lives from other dimensions that frequently enter into this one—and even scare them at times. We need to awaken you to this eventuality now. If you are afraid of other aspects of your personality and soul, you cannot accept other relationships. If your relationship to your body is stretched and sagging beyond belief, why would you be keen on knowing about other personal aspects?

We know you all wonder about your dreams and where they come from, so we will not delay working on them. We will enter your dreams, as will your Spirit Guides and others from the higher realms, but mostly your dreams are of the world you live in *versus* the world where you have another life to live—and acknowledge within *you*. This other world exists as much as this one, but you do not enter it that often. In your sleep there are many more opportunities to enter the mind of a personality than in waking hours when there is much commotion around or within you.

The world of dreams is solitary, but not confined. It is a world of deep dreams with lots of activity. It is not the design of someone else or anything unknown, rather yours alone. You weave patterns into dreams you can change or alter at will. If your life here is boring, you weave exciting dreams. If your present life is too hectic, you dream of pastures, lakes, and water to calm you. If your love life is still—not stimulating, you will not dream of love—but lust. If you cannot lust after others and have a fear of love, you will dream of fairytale-type romances and read such books. You will not be afraid in such a dream and may even erupt into true passion one day.

Whatever your dreams mean to you, you are not the only one sharing that dream! Many people believe they have their own private dream—which is not true. You have to share. You have to learn to live together, and many refuse to do it on a physical level, so you do it in a spiritual form. The only time some meet others is in your dreams. If you fear the opposite sex in this life, for whatever reason, you may not even see them in your dreams. We work to free you of such fear. Once you can meet fears in your dreams, you are free of them.

Nightmares are dreams of fear and trials of flesh that evil-minded individuals are prone to have. You need not condemn yourself if you have such dreams, but you should recognize them as being manifested by you—not God or someone else. If your dreams are troublesome, your life is not going smoothly—regardless of what you say.

Many things in a dream evolve into other events, people, and activities, but you may not realize it now. One dream seemingly flows into another, yet all concern the same subject. The first dream creates the second, and so on.

If your dreams are not of this world, you may not realize it. The other planets are not like Earth, but you are. You see, taste, and hear things, but may not hear much while on Earth. On other planets hearing is more acute. You can begin to understand this if you listen as a dog does to sounds all around you. You may be deaf after a lifetime on Earth, but dogs carry a high incidence of acute hearing with them to their deaths.

We confuse some of you, because we skip around, but it all comes together in the end. You have to pay attention! We do it to confuse fools. Fools seek only sensational material to absorb and use to control others or gain money, so we confound them here. It is easy to do. You, too, can do it and should.

There are many people around you in the world now. You have a lot of noise to contend with, so you do not listen. Instead you become numb—and then you die. Do you see how it diminishes *you*? Whatever you do, do not turn up the volume of sound until it hurts your ears. The ear is the most valuable of all your senses. Great hearing ability is required to define the design of the spheres.

If a lower species, such as dogs, has a greater degree of hearing than any human, why would you worry? We know of people who hold séances and ask to hear raps and knocks. Why? Spirits of those departed are not going to rap or knock. They can, but why should they? Dogs could talk, but why should they? You can walk and talk, but not hear much. Why should you? Because your ego thinks it knows all there is to know now, even though you do not know much about anything.

Remember to remain humble!

To remain humble is better than to act like a fool who believes she or he knows all there is to know about everything. Some areas of business or industry can be absorbed and completely known, but not the areas involving people. No person has ever learned to know another. It is an interesting pastime to try, but not one that pays well.

People who know the ways of the world often make more money than those of a more spiritual nature, and you may wonder why. Simple! You now base your assumptions on one set of principles versus another and cannot compute. To define ego is to assert you know who you are. To define Spirit is to believe. We know of no one on Earth so far who knows who *'this self'* is, but many strive to find out. You need to discover who is close to the end of this search and learn from them.

Work on self is not a full-time job, but it can be absorbing enough to take you away from your everyday work. You need to work daily to earn your keep and keep your own from want. Whatever work you do on *you* is given total commitment by the realms above, but you are not helped with it. You first earn each step of the way, then you are blessed with *Gifts of The Holy Spirit*.

To study psychology or science in order to learn about being human is a waste of time. If you meditate, it all makes sense and you learn much quicker. Most students are lazy and do not want to meditate, but it is the key to all knowledge. If you cannot listen, you will not learn. If you refuse to learn, you will die and return, return, and return to this work until you do learn. Meditate now and get it over with forever!

Whenever you make some lame excuse for not meditating, you look foolish. Because of this lack of commitment, you will not be given any *psychic ability* (as you call it) or any other ability to control or predict your future. It is not learnable—you have to earn it. Whatever you do to learn a skill, you have to practice it over and over until you know it, but with *Gifts from The Holy Spirit*, you instantly *know*.

Working on your life is the best way to advance and succeed. If you try to improve others—leaving your life in chaos, you will fail. No one listens to those not working out their life needs. It takes failure to determine whether or not the price is worth the pain. Once you know what you *really* want from this life, you can move ahead. Most people spend at least half their lives making a mess of it and the other half straightening it out. Why live that way? Why not enjoy all there is to know and have a great life, too? It is as easy to do as making a mess of it!

The only job in this world worthy of *you* is your spiritual life. You need to begin enjoying it now and secure all the love you can while still here. Love streams around you daily, but few attempt to gain it now.

Work is not love, but love works. You can find work you love or work you hate, so why work at what you hate? Of course, this is always your decision.

What you need to know before you marry anyone, or even live together, is what degree of commitment *you*—not the other person— have made to the relationship. We see so many ask if the other party is committed to the relationship. Why? It matters not if the other party loves, if you do not. Why would it matter if the other party does not love, if you do? It is not a waste of energy or time to love, rather the growth of Spirit within you. Let it flow. Let it grow. Let it have a life of its own and enjoy yourself while you are 'in love.' Later you can enjoy the pleasures of knowing the other party also loves you. If the other party does not and never will love you, transfer that emotion to another who can. Not so difficult to figure out. Is it?

We want you to know why you select certain people for sex or lust rather than love. We know many men are filled with lust and share no love with anyone. They lust after a man or woman—and not care which. To know love—not lust is to share the joys and sorrows of this life with another. Lust is just lust. It has no depth or joy beyond the sensual source.

If you believe you have only one life to live, why would you live it with another? Why not live alone and enjoy everything you earn or produce? Because deep within you, you know you came here to multiply and divide. You know you are here to learn to live with others of the same background, as well as learn to tolerate all others, even though you do not exactly remember the goal. Exact memory comes to those who work on it, but few do.

When you are at a loss for words, do you cry? Do you fear? Do you ask for mercy? No, you say: *"I don't know what to say."* It is this simple to ask for help, say aloud, *"I need _____."* Your needs are fulfilled early, and as efficiently as possible. If you say instead: *"I want _____,"* you may have a long wait. It is not the desire of those above to give you all you want now. Spoiling a personality is not the way to develop character.

Child-rearing is the most difficult of all jobs on Earth, and most of you are failing at it now. Why? It was mastered once, but you let it fall into disarray. Why? Ego! You believe you know everything. You believe your ways are better than those of your elders. You think you are better than they are. Since it is such a difficult subject, in the future we will dedicate an entire book to child-raising, but for now—listen to your elders. They knew how to raise children, and most likely you do not.

If your life is full of joy, how can anyone hate you? Simple! If your friends are actually enemies, you can have no safety from envy, jealousy, and collusion among them. You must be very selective about who you let come close to you. Wise women and men are selective about their friends, because they cannot easily determine who is friend or foe, so how can children know? It is the duty of adults to shield them as much as possible from evil, but not prevent them from learning as early as possible the skills needed to be a successful adult—and learning quickly who your friends are is an essential skill.

In order to be selective, you need to know about the work of other people. If they do not work, you should stay clear. If their work is less than agreeable, stay to see if they change it. If they work at honorable tasks and chores, doing them as well as they can, they will stick by you, too.

When you get to know a person, you know only the exterior persona. If you pray for that person, you may know them better—but maybe not. While on Earth it is not your business to know the inner person—but when you cross over to the other side it is. If you learn to internally understand others at least part of the time, you are on the other side. Such experience may come to you through dreams or during meditation.

Dreams are where we began this session and where we will end it, but now we want to again explore meditation for a brief spell. You learn many things while meditating, but may not be aware you are. The heart beats and lungs breathe, but your mind is in limbo (as you describe it—not us) and you do not remember. We will help you remember what is important.

If you wish to remember a point, mentally take note of it. Say to yourself: *"I need to remember this for future use,"* and it is done! You can retrieve it later. If you make no such notation, you will forget it almost immediately. We want you to be able to retrieve much of the information you gain through meditation, thus we suggest you announce your intention each time you initiate a meditation session. Put your life on hold and ask only for the blessing of memory. It will take place and not clutter your conscious mind—then if you need it, it is there.

The Scribe can easily channel other people's Spiritual Guides—and does it accurately, but she retains no memory of it afterwards. She requested this initially because she has no desire to remember the private lives of others. She is wise. You need not remember anything about others' lives, either. It is best to keep your life simple, so you can remember it later.

Putting your life on hold so it can mend is an acceptable practice, but it requires much energy. If you have no energy, you cannot meditate. Surprises you? We believe you think meditation is a time of rest, but it is not.

You work hard during meditation

It is difficult to ascertain how much energy you use when meditating, but it adds up to a substantial amount. You burn fat to heat the body and move it, but burn minerals and vitamins to exercise the mind. If your body had as many things going on at one time as your mind, you would be dead within minutes of birth. Do not starve the mind, rather eat for it as well as the body.

The fish of your seas once contained many fats and minerals, but not today. Your vegetables once contained minerals and vitamins that no longer exist in the soil. You have depleted Earth of these various elements with no remorse, but the body will suffer and is already showing signs of increased stress and strain caused by a lack of certain important minerals it requires.

To counteract the overflow of your waste into the waters of the world and Earth itself, you must sift through your body from time-to-time and deposit waste elsewhere. You refer to this process as cleansing, but we call it eliminating the evil from within the body. Whatever you call it, it needs to be done regularly.

More than enough time has been spent channeling this material, but few recognize that, for personal reasons, some control it and make it unavailable to the masses. If your greed keeps you from channeling your ideas to others now, you will not be allowed to benefit from it in the future.

Psychics know of many healings, but do not tell why they occurred or any of the facts behind them, in order to avoid penalty of the law. This is not the same as denial, but it serves the same purpose. To know what to do is not as desirable as being willing to do it.

Most health regimes are arduous only to the person needing it. Others with no such problem could accomplish it easily, but that is why they do not have that particular problem. You need to decide once and for all to rid yourself of a particular vice and then do it!

If you have no mind, you cannot understand what you are doing or saying, but your brain might record it anyway. What you say is not as important as how you mean it. Nice words in foul mouths are not heard as positive, but evil words spoken by seemingly nice people does much damage. Do not ever use your energy to do evil. If you did, let it go.

The power of evil to multiply is no different from positive energy sources. It can control you or not. It is your decision. It is created by you and lasts as long as you feed it. To eventually let evil thoughts consume your life is to give yourself over to evil that once was. No one now knows of that time, but it did exist.

We are not here to dwell on evil or negativity since it increases fear. Fear is the evil you promote most and cannot rid yourself of now. Do not let anyone ever edge you over to the other side of reasoning. Remain steadfast and true to your inner being—remain calm and cool. All fear disappears in the presence of calm, cool reason.

In the dreams of your sleep are times when fear controls you. You need to learn to remain calm and cool when this occurs. Do not let a dream override your conscious life. You will be unable to determine if true or not, so let it go. Never dwell on the negative! It has no validity in this world. It is the evil you produce while dwelling in this world's negativity that produces crime and other social ills—not God chastising you all.

We will go no further into the dream world, since you need to know so much more about relationships, but we will help you come to terms with those dreams that produce negative feelings in your conscious being. The following exercises are meant to be taped and used to reprogram your mind in order to rid your dreams of evil or negative thoughts.

Complete these exercises now, and again later in life. Each time you do them, your dreams should improve. If a dream state is interfered with, it can drive you to distraction. Also, be careful when talking about your dreams, because they contain much information about your personal life and could be used by unscrupulous people to expose your frailties.

EXERCISES IN DREAMING

1. As you go to sleep, place a tablet beside you and let your mind fill its pages later. If you write down every word, your mind cannot escape scrutiny. It will try to avoid details, but you can prevent that by first remembering your dream in its entirety before moving a muscle—then start writing. Be sure to use little light so your eyes are not completely awakened or hurt by the intensity.
2. If you have a tape recorder, initially put your dreams on tape, then write them in a dream journal later. You need a long time to record all the symbols in your dreams, so begin by using universal symbols reported by others. After you record each dream, circle the universal symbols such as water, clouds, horses, people, numbers, etc. Circle them until you receive meanings of your own. To begin analyzing dreams before you know even one symbol's meaning is a waste. Let them accumulate as you build your glossary of dream meanings.
3. Put your mind into the act of writing down your dreams. When you finish writing out a dream, always ask what the

dream means. You may be told immediately! Your hand may even continue writing and reveal its meaning or the symbolic meaning of the dream, but you need to ask for that.

4. A dream is given to you to use. Each time, ask why it was given to you. If you fail to ask, you may never find out why it came to you then. All dreams are to be used! If you know immediately why you had the dream, you can immediately develop it. Always ask why it came to you and how you can best use it now and in the future.

5. Pull covers over your head and ask aloud if clouds will only be overhead or scattered. If the clouds of the next day or that morning are in agreement with what you were told, you know the source of your dreams is accurate. Predictions must be verified!

6. To deny you dream is a fiction no one believes; but some do not remember dreams. It is their mind's way of ignoring all things spiritual. If your mind has no way to tell you of your future, how can you prepare for it? No way can you be prepared, unless you seek out someone to channel your inner sources. Meditate on your dreams daily. Why be dependent upon others when you can do it yourself?

7. Put your mind into creating your next dream. Upon retiring, say: *"I am able to dream. I will remember all of my dreams. I need to know about* _____." Your next dream sequence will identify the key elements about the subject in doubt. You will know what to do, but may not wish to remember it or follow through and do it. In time you will learn to trust dream work as giving you great advice.

When you seek out another to interpret a dream, you seek out someone to do your spiritual work. This is not the best way to learn, and it can foul your system. Initially a dream interpreter can help you learn about dreams and develop a dictionary of symbols, but after that you need to do such work alone if you are to grow spiritually from it.

Respecting your dreams is the ultimate goal of this chapter. If you learned only that one thing, we have succeeded in helping you identify a source of wisdom always readily available to you. It is your decision whether or not you use it. We could elaborate upon symbols, and dreams others have had, but it does not mean much to you. Your dreams are *your* dreams. We will help you in your dreams, if you wish, but normally we help you through others' work, which you can read or hear about.

The time is now here when you need to begin using all these chapters to develop a better means of relating to others within your world. If your dreams of another world can help, we will be glad to help you. If your dreams of another world are not of any use in this one, we will ignore them, too.

Dreaming is not easy to understand and acknowledge, but to deny you dream is stupid and unforgivable from the standpoint of recognizing who you are. People hate to admit they trust their dreams, but most do once they understand them. It is easy to understand some dreams, but quite difficult to come to a *total understanding* of one. Be careful of your time on Earth and not waste too much of it on dreams—since they are from other worlds.

Chapter **Twenty**

The only one of three rules you are expected to never break is: Do no evil to anyone! Nevertheless, it is often broken. The only way to avoid doing evil is to think no evil, which is where most humans go wrong. You believe that if you think evil of someone and never say a word aloud you will avoid trouble, but you cannot think it and never do it.

It works this way: First you see, then you want—then you ask and receive. If you do not see anything, you do not want. If you have no wants, you cannot ask. If you never ask, you do not receive. The work of this world is not as easy as that, but it does operate much the way you would expect if you had no problems within *you*.

The real problem now is that almost everyone has serious problems within them which resulted in their appearance here on Earth. If the problems are not resolved, the return to Earth is extended. To extend a life on Earth for several episodes to solve one problem usually operates on the basis that life is not easy here and you need more time; however, some come back to enjoy the fruits of their earlier labors or to earn additional points.

If your life is long on Earth, you will know many things about the world, but be careful! You can become so entrapped by the negativity here that you cannot free yourself. To be free of negativity in a world built around it is a difficult task, but one which many can accomplish.

You must be clear. Clearing your mind daily helps, and having others around you who are clear will extend your field; but if you have trouble doing it, ask for help. We are not able to cleanse the field or increase your power, but others can and will do it do it for you if you ask.

Why would you need to be cleansed? You are not negative or able to work in negativity long. You need to be freed of its drain on your positive ions or become sick from it. When you say you feel drained, you are referring to your energy level. You do feel drained. It is an apt description. You cannot afford to let others drain you. If you find a certain person repeatedly does this, fend them off and remove them from your life.

If your life on Earth is not full of positive episodes, you may say you are being drained, which is incorrect. You create these episodes on Earth and are thus responsible for their outcomes—both good and bad. If you fear anyone or anything, you created it—so remove it. If you are unhappy to be here, that is your decision and cannot be blamed on others. If your life is going nowhere, you are the only one to know where it should go. If you think you will not be loved, you will never be loved.

It is no big secret how life works, but you may not be doing your work. If your work in this world is unfulfilling, you can either do more or less and add or subtract from it, but you cannot refuse to work. The only people free of physical work are disabled—and disability is not a lifetime excuse. The body will free itself of pain, if permitted, but it may take a long time. If your mind is full of pain, it can take an entire lifetime to free itself, but it can be done. You need to first decide whether your pain is mental, physical, or spiritual, then prepare to hurt no more. This is a decision—and you make it. Once the decision is made, the pain will ease up until it is gone. It may take years, but it will disappear.

You need to believe in YOU. If you believe in God, you believe in YOU. If you do not believe in God, you cannot believe in *you*, either. The basics are always so simple.

If your life is such that you cannot understand where you are now, you may have suggested to yourself that you will never know. The question should be: Do I know who I am? If you do not, you cannot know where to go.

In the deep recesses of the heart are many memories of years ago and ages ago which cannot help you now. If you can forget these old memories, you can walk forward. If you resolve each life as you live it, you can move forward. It is dragging the past forward which slows the mind. You need to free yourself of this bad habit now.

Work is not going to help you if you never see it as a remedy. If your mind is sore, read. If your spirit is ill, meditate. If your back hurts, do not work with a shovel. Concentrate on what hurts—then repeat the above.

Placing your hand in front of your eyes does not prevent you from seeing, but never looking into your heart will. You need to develop a way to see without using your eyes. The greatest method known to men of Earth to secure what they need is visualization, but so few use it that we can only wonder why.

Pulling your back up and arching it is not the way to un-kink your spine, but many persistently do this and injure their backs. You have to breathe into the spine and let it do its own *un-kinking*. If you let the spine deliberately *un-kink*, it will. While you take in breath, let up on the pressure—letting oxygen ease into the tissue. Once that breath is gone and you cannot feel it, breathe in again and again until you relax.

We will help all who ask for help in healing. It is not difficult to heal the body or mind. It is your spirit that needs help. You cannot ask the mind to heal the body, but Spirit can. If your body is well and able to function, and the mind is, too, you may or may not be happy. Your spirit is not necessarily connected to both. You must connect it.

Working on You is of The Holy Spirit and requires you to acknowledge you have a goal. If you have none, your life is a farce requiring no planning. If your life requires no planning, you need not bother to work. If you do not work, you may as well have not come to Earth.

Working for *you* is the work of Spiritual Guides, but not all of them are here to work. Some of your Guides are here to seek out a new life for the rest of your being. Remember, you have a large network of beings within your soul. If one of the other dimensions within your soul is in dire need, all the Guides for all the entities within your soul come to the rescue. If you do not intend to listen to their wisdom, calling all your Spiritual Guides is a waste of energy.

Always welcome your Guides!

If you feel nothing, you are yet unable to understand. If you can hear or feel their presence, you may ask for help. If you already know your Spiritual Guides, they will immediately help you. The time to establish a lasting connection with them is when you do not need help. If you wait until you are in dire pain to connect, you risk not hearing their advice and continuing to suffer.

Working for The High Guides is often the way to get better. You can help those whom The High Guides are working on then. If you think positive thoughts and seldom ask for help, the energy you would have drained from your total being is transferred to others within your soul. Since the others are in spirit, it is not a big, elaborate network. You are the only one in flesh residing in a negative atmosphere.

Your life is unlike the life of anyone else. If you had a lot of time on Earth, you would never finish your work, so you stay only a relatively short time. If the time is too short, you will come back. In the past it was not a problem to be returned to Earth, but now it is—and must be reversed.

You have to seek access to the next plane or be lost. To be lost does not mean you wander around on Earth. Your planet is about to be void of life. You have cut off all air and water, which humans require, and emptied the Earth of most of its contents. This imbalance cannot prevent you from advancing, but it will most likely cause the planet to shoot off its orbit and disintegrate while there is still life on it. In either case, life cannot return.

Pulling your own cart is the best way to advance. If you ask other people to help you, you will have to repay them. If you ask for help from the higher realms, you will receive much more help and not have to repay it. Putting all your energy into one project is also not wise. If you are to work all your life, you need several avenues of work.

The only people who are not expected to work are shamans. If you are a shaman, you already work spiritually, so you do not need physical work, but most shamans are also workers. Working within the Spirit is the most difficult of all tasks. Have you tried for years of this life to meditate and not had much success? Think of the shamans who meditate and work at the same time. How can you do that, too? Work at it!

If you envy shamans, you will not be one

Envy kills any good person's inspiration and creates evil. You need not want to be a shaman to be one, but it helps. If your life is over now and you have no one, you may decide to retreat from life and dedicate yourself to God, but that is unwise. You should begin early in life to dedicate your work to God—then shamanic robes will be placed upon you.

For every person who works hard at life, there are several who only play at it. Why would the upper planes help? All who live on Earth are seekers and need guidance. If a seeker never helps others, the Earth is diminished, but not God. If the seeker learns to help others, Earth is extended, but not God. God is not of Earth. God created Earth.

Your life here is not your life. You have nothing in *you* that can be enhanced by this life, but your other parts enhance this life. To not recognize you are related to several beings within one soul is to not know who *you* are.

This is the final chapter about relationships, thus it needs to be thoroughly understood before any further training can be given. If your life here is incomplete, you will not be allowed to advance to the next plane. If you can absorb what your relationship is to all present here and above, you will advance. Your life depends upon understanding all the relationships that exist within and outside *you*.

You cannot shirk this work!

You will know if you are the only one within You to live on Earth. Your Guides are of Spirit and have knowledge they can use to help you. If your Spiritual Guides never dwelled on Earth, your knowledge is theoretical and not easily understood by *you*. If your Guides lived on Earth, their help is more practical. You cannot know if your Guides lived on Earth or not, unless you called upon them and were given help. Whether your Guides help you or not is not the question. The question is: Do you know you have Spiritual Guides?

Many of Earth's inhabitants are scared of their own being. They think their spiritual self is evil. They fear each other. They cannot grasp why they are here on Earth. They know not one another. They fear God. They are unaware of God, and not *'of God'* in anything they do. What can you do about it? Simple—pray for them!

You are not blessed if you know of God, but you can be blessed. At times you must do your own blessing, for God is not on Earth. You live in this world in order to learn to develop fully and become *of God*. If you had God at hand, you would never learn. The Spiritual Guides of higher realms are always available, and help at all times, but God is not to be called by you.

The only time you will know God is when you no longer are you. If you believe you know God now, you display egotism. Egoism is the bane of the world in which you live now, but understandable. You do not know much, so you become superstitious and fear those who do know God. You blame God, because you cannot fathom *you* are You. It is not mature to blame others—especially God, but it is the way of your present world to do so.

We are not here to judge you, but there will be a time when you are judged, and it may not be pleasant. Be prepared. Once in a place of judgment, it is too late to repent, but you can repent now. Repent of the past and let it go.

Get your life in order now and the future is great. We know of no one denied entrance to the next plane who has not repented. Confused? Look at your life. Do you say, *"I'm sorry?"* Of course you do. Are you sorry? Most likely you are not. Do you repent? Seldom is one asked this question, because it is deep, but it is valid. Did you ever truly repent anything? Fear is what prevents you from renouncing all you did that may have harmed anyone. You fear you will never be able to reenter your soul if you leave it for even a second, but you still do it. You do not actually leave your soul, but you frequently abandon it.

We seek only those who have loved and been loved. If your life is devoid of love, you cannot love. We will never bother to learn all your ways, because we do not have time for that, but you know your ways, so ask us for help.

When you seek love, you seek a means to establish a relationship within you and God. It does not work. God is not within a relationship of two humans. You cannot know God by marrying another human or having sex.

It is extremely embarrassing to have to announce this now, since it is so very obvious, but there are certain religious people who piously believe they are uniting with God when they couple. This is an outrageous belief! You cannot experience God. It is not possible. You live on Earth, dwelling in the afterlife of a beautiful planet destroyed by you and those before you, but you do not *know* God.

If your life on Earth is successful and you grow to the next plane, we cannot help you then. If you remain here, your life will be in mortal jeopardy, but we can still help you. Our relationship to you is temporary. We will leave this plane before the final destruction, but until then we work here. If you advance, others of another order will help you there and above that plane. You will never be without help! It is your life. You have to develop or die, but you have help moving your life upward and into the full being of God.

If your life is not presently flowing, you can ask us for help, but your Spiritual Guides can help you even more, since they will be with *you* when you cross over to a higher plane. Your Guides are held responsible for helping *you*. They are not punished if you do not do what they advise, but you are punished if you do not do it.

Guides help others, in order to advance. You will be asked, too, if you achieve the next plane, to guide others left here. It is an ongoing process, but one which establishes you as being of God or not.

To determine if you are *'not of God'* requires a lot of deep explanation and will be covered—but not here right now. You cannot absorb everything. You cannot learn everything, but you can try. Any attempt to help *you* results in a better soul. If your entire being strives to do better, you will ultimately unite with God. If your entire being does not strive to live the best it can, your soul may be destroyed. This is a matter of importance to all, but only *you* can prevent such a serious mission being aborted. Your life here is no measure of who *you* are, but it indicates the direction your soul is taking now. You will know.

The following exercises conclude the work on relationships, but such work will never be complete. You can always work on it. This work continues even beyond Earth.

EXERCISES ON PREPARING TO MEET GOD

1. THE ONLY TIME YOU WILL KNOW GOD IS WHEN YOU ARE OF GOD! WORKING ON GOD IS FORBIDDEN, BUT WORKING ON SELF IS NECESSARY. YOU ARE NEVER LOST AND ABANDONED, BUT YOU MUST WORK. ASK—WE CAN HELP YOU NOW.
2. PUTTING YOURSELF IN FIRST PLACE RESULTS IN DEMOTION. PUT YOURSELF IN THE BEST POSSIBLE POSITION FOR ADVANCEMENT OF YOUR SOUL, AND FORGET ABOUT ADVANCEMENT OF YOUR CAREER OR LIFE ON EARTH. IT AUTOMATICALLY COMES TO THOSE WHO WORK. TO PLACE YOURSELF WELL, SIMPLY MEDITATE EVERY DAY.
3. PLAN TO BE *YOU* EVERY DAY OF YOUR LIFE—WITH NO EXCEPTIONS.

4. BEGIN EACH DAY WITH PRAISE AND END IT THE SAME WAY.

5. ASK FOR HELP WE ASSURED YOU IS YOURS FOR THE ASKING. DO NOT ASK OTHERS FOR HELP, INSTEAD ASK YOUR GUIDES OR US. IF YOUR NEEDS ARE NOT MET, YOU CANNOT BE FREE. WE WANT YOU TO BE FREE OF WANT IN ORDER TO BE.

6. PULL OUT OF ANY ARRANGEMENTS WHERE YOU ARE NOT *YOU*. ENTER INTO NO FUTURE PARTNERSHIPS WHERE YOU CANNOT BE *YOU*. LIVE AS YOU ARE—NOT AS YOU THINK OTHERS WANT YOU TO LIVE. LOOK AT EACH PERSON YOU MEET AS THOUGH A FRIEND. LOOK FOR THE BEST IN EACH OF THESE MEETINGS. SERVE GOD IN AS MANY WAYS AS POSSIBLE. NEVER WORRY ABOUT THE MEANS TO AN END—JUST THE END.

7. WE CAN NEVER ANSWER ALL YOUR QUESTIONS, BUT YOU HAVE ALL THE ANSWERS TO YOUR QUESTIONS. *ASK YOU!* YOU NEED ONLY GO WITHIN DURING MEDITATION TO LEARN ALL THERE IS TO KNOW.

(THE SCRIBE IS CONSTANTLY TRYING TO SWITCH TO LOWER-CASE LETTERS AND UNABLE TO DO SO, BECAUSE THE POWER OF THIS MESSAGE IS SUCH THAT THE MACHINE UPON WHICH SHE TYPES CANNOT HANDLE IT. CAN YOU?)

WORK FOR THE DAY WHEN YOU ARE

NO LONGER ON EARTH,

LIVE FOR NOW AND YOU LIVE ALWAYS!

THESE ARE OUR LAST WORDS UNTIL WE MEET AGAIN.

May 6, 1994
(Reexamined July 2016)
Ruth Lee, Scribe to The Teachers of The Higher Planes

End Notes

Teachers open the door, you enter by yourself!
--Ancient Chinese Proverb

In Chapter Four of this book you were given work to do and instructed to place your findings here. That text is repeated for your convenience:

At the end of this book list the titles of books you can access at the local library to develop your social perspective and psychology relative to living with others. We suggest you seek books that can help you understand your life now...Include a few books that are not new—have been around for ages, because wisdom is not likely to go out of style. Read and reread anything that helps you develop your personality so it accepts your spiritual nature....

We suggest you seek books that can help you understand your life now. Once you study the basics of social psychology you need only brush up on it from time-to-time as more is learned about the psychology of relationships,. If you never studied psychology and have had problems with relationships in the past, you know already to include other areas of study, too.

You are now left to work on your own to build healthy, loving, lasting relationships wherever you may be. Good Luck!

Everything you need to know relative to the other areas of your life here on Earth and elsewhere is covered in other volumes of *The Books of Wisdom* from **The Teachers of The Higher Planes**. To read more about *The Teachers* as well as their scribe, Ruth Lee, go to: www.LeeWayPublishing.com

Have You Read...
We Are Here

There is more to living and dying than human beings see while on Earth. Are you aware that intelligent beings who exist beyond our time and space are working diligently to teach universal truths? Well, there are, and they are here now!

We Are Here ~ *The Teachers of the Higher Planes* is the work of those charged with educating humanity on the basic facts of life, including spirituality and ascension. Through their scribe, Ruth Lee, material essential to living a full and meaningful life is presented in easy-to-read prose guaranteed to open your mind to what exists around us at all times.

Created for those who wonder about the fundamental questions of life: Who am I? Why am I here? Are we alone? **We Are Here ~ *The Teachers of the Higher Planes*** provides the answers!

In plain, everyday language *The Teachers* lay bare aspects of our world which endanger mankind—and even Earth itself. In this, the first volume in the ***Books of Wisdom*** series, they provide a blue print and clear instructions on how to correct the problems of our times and ascend at the end.

We Are Here ~ *The Teachers of the Higher Planes* is a must read for every serious spiritual seeker. For more information on **We Are Here** and the other ***Books of Wisdom***, as well as Ruth Lee, Scribe, visit: *www.LeeWayPublishing.com*

www.ingramcontent.com/pod-product-compliance
Lightning Source LLC
Chambersburg PA
CBHW052035090426
42739CB00010B/1924